JOSÉ 'Pepe' MUJICA

From Montevideo, Uruguay,
home of José 'Pepe' Mujica,
where the author now lives with his wife Lilian,
he dedicates this book to his children
Myra in Sydney, Australia
and **Warren** on Victoria Island, Canada

JOSÉ 'Pepe' MUJICA
WARRIOR   PHILOSOPHER   PRESIDENT

STEPHEN GREGORY

sussex
ACADEMIC
PRESS
Brighton • Portland • Toronto

2 4 6 8 10 9 7 5 3 1

First published in hardcover 2016 in Great Britain by
SUSSEX ACADEMIC PRESS
PO Box 139, Eastbourne BN24 9BP

Distributed in North America by
SUSSEX ACADEMIC PRESS
ISBS Publisher Services
920 NE 58th Ave #300, Portland, OR 97213, USA

British Library Cataloguing in Publication Data
A CIP catalogue record for this book is available from the British Library.

Library of Congress Cataloging-in-Publication Data
Names: Gregory, Stephen, 1948, author.
Title: Jose 'Pepe' Mujica: warrior, philosopher, president / Stephen Gregory.
Other titles: Jose 'Pepe' Mujica, warrior, philosopher, president
Description: Chicago : Sussex Academic Press, [2016] | Includes index.
Identifiers: LCCN 2015047054| ISBN 9781845197896 (pbk : alk. paper) |
    ISBN 9781782843054 (mobi) | ISBN 9781782843061 (pdf)
Subjects: LCSH: Mujica Cordano, Jose Alberto, 1934– | Uruguay—Politics
    and government—1985– | Presidents—Uruguay—Biography.
Classification: LCC F2729.52.M85 G74 2016 | DDC 989.506/7092—dc23
LC record available at http://lccn.loc.gov/2015047054

Typeset & designed by Sussex Academic Press, Brighton & Eastbourne.

Contents

Preface   vi
Acknowledgements   xi

Introduction
A Portly Knight and His Far From Average First Lady   1

Chapter One
WARRIOR   7
Flower Power   7
A Political Apprenticeship   16
Fire Power   23

Chapter Two
PHILOSOPHER   44
A Tupamaro Persona?   45
The Left Before Taking Power   56
Horizontal and Egalitarian or Vertical and Hierarchical?   69
Parliament and the Problem of Representation   74

Chapter Three
PRESIDENT   79
Uruguay after the Deluge   81
From Deputy and Senator to Minister   86
The Presidency and After   97

Conclusion
A Left Alternative?   109
The Philosopher Takes Power while the Politician Thinks   110
What is Left?   126

Glossary   132
Chronology   140
Sources   146
Index   151

Preface

What follows is written by an Anglo-Australian academic Latin Americanist who has a specialist interest in the involvement of Uruguayan intellectuals in their country's political affairs and who, now retired from university administration, teaching and research, lives in the Uruguayan capital, reads its press and watches its television. Two earlier books by the author, detailed in the Bibliography, have provided background material for the current writing.

This brief volume is not academic. The material is not footnoted and is not the product of new research. Quite the contrary. It rehashes already published material, almost all of it from Uruguay and in Spanish. What lies at its core is the author's belief that the relevance of José 'Pepe' Mujica in the modern world far exceeds that of the eccentrically dressed national president who took the global media by storm at venues such as the United Nations and World Environment summits with largely improvised fiery speeches on such topics as the dangers to human life posed by rampant consumerism, continued environmental vandalism and unimpeded industrially produced climate change. Interviews often conducted in the then President's humble, picturesquely shambolic semi-rural home and published in newspapers, magazines and websites in many languages throughout the world showed how Mujica and his wife (also an active politician) contributed by example both at home and at work to illustrating how it was possible to live comfortably but modestly while doing what one could to mitigate these ills. And all of this while being now aging survivors of guerrilla war, political imprisonment and a military dictatorship's torture chambers.

This is more than enough to justify the interest of the world's media in the head of government of one of the planet's smallest nations that usually only figures in the international press when its widely exported best soccer players do something noteworthy. However, José 'Pepe' Mujica's importance is much more closely related to his political activities at home than is indicated in recent media headlines abroad. Consequently, the book seeks to situate for the non-specialist English-language reader the figure of Mujica in his native Uruguayan context in order to suggest the potential relevance of his activities and thinking to the international revival of a Left alternative after the collapse of so-called 'existing socialism' in 1989–90 led to the subsequent apparently unstoppable rise and spread of globalised market economics and its accomplice capitalist democracy. For Mujica and increasing numbers of others, this seemingly invincible and self-righteous couple are largely if not entirely responsible for the situations he has felt called upon to denounce and (where possible) alter, as well as for others such as what BBC World, as I write this in September 2015, is calling the 'European migrant crisis' brought about by refugees from civil wars raging in Syria, Iraq and Libya and the accompanying unprincipled and opportunistic (and not infrequently tragic) international trade in illegal people trafficking.

It is this context of the resurgence of reformulated left-wing options that Mujica's politics and its attendant thinking that is introduced by the first two of the six epigraphs that precede the Introduction. The last four are one-liners from the man who is at the centre of the pages to follow and will find any necessary explanation or justification there. The first two, however, require some brief elucidation. Mario Benedetti, like Mujica, was a lowly listed candidate for the People's Union, a coalition built around the youthful and more unconventional sector of the Uruguayan Socialist Party, which received minuscule electoral support in the 1962 national elections and resulted in the Socialist Party, whose respectable and mildly successful existence dated from 1910, having no representation in the Parliament resulting from the ballot. Benedetti, a popular and critically acclaimed writer of fiction, poetry and essays, cynically disillusioned regarding the left's chances of enlisting support in an electoral system designed to keep out intruders who threatened to disrupt the political status quo, gave an invited talk to the Socialist Party faithful in May 1963 in which he advised the left to steer clear of the corrupt Uruguayan democratic system but concluded that the left had to make the choice summed up in the quoted sentence: unite around the lengthy task of preparing for a genuine revolution or drastically revise its strategy and tactics if it wanted to persevere with electoral democracy Uruguayan style. Mujica, equally disillusioned, opted for the first of these choices and got closer to what in 1964 would reveal itself as the (in)famous Tupamaros National Liberation Movement, the guerrilla group that would be a protagonist in the Uruguayan political scene until its final defeat in the second half of 1972, leading to dictatorship for the whole nation, imprisonment and exile for many, death for more than just a few, and torture, solitary confinement and a period of near insanity for Mujica himself. After release in 1985, both Mujica and the much-transformed Tupamaros would finally adopt the second option offered by Benedetti back in 1963, but in the very changed post-dictatorial circumstances of the 1980s. Benedetti himself had tried to have the best of both worlds, co-founding in 1971 a legal organisation that was in effect the Tupamaros guerrilla's legal shop front while also participating in the fledgling united left's Broad Front coalition that got a respectable eighteen percent of the vote in that year's national elections, the last before the military coup in June 1973. The price Benedetti paid for his militancy was twelve years of enforced exile in Argentina, Peru, Cuba and Spain, returning to Uruguay at roughly the same time Mujica was released from jail.

The relevance of the second epigraph, from an essay by French philosopher Alain Badiou, may be less immediately apparent but is no less direct, though in a very different way. Badiou is one of the figures most closely associated with a philosophical re-founding of the left in the developed world. He calls this new phenomenon "Communism" but it has nothing to do with what has been associated with the word in the twentieth century. Rather, it is the name in inverted commas Badiou gives to a current that is still to be realised but whose very basic coordinates he has been interested in suggesting in works such as *The Communist Hypothesis* and the one quoted here, *Philosophy for Militants*. At other moments in the book, readers will find Mujica's name associated with that of French-Algerian and Jewish philosopher Jacques Derrida, who has always claimed to be a man of the left (although many of his readers have found it difficult to accept) much of whose later work, such as *The Politics of Friendship* and *Specters of Marx*, was concerned to build the outlines of a new ethical politics or political ethics based on the assumption established in his earlier literary philosophy that the truth exists but is accessible to language only as trope and not as fact or point of reference that can be reliably grounded outside a language framework. Both these sophisticated academic thinkers may seem far removed from the largely autodidact and practical militant that is Mujica, but in this case appearances really are deceptive.

There are two fundamental principles that Mujica shares with both Badiou and Derrida: first, all three affirm in their different ways the necessary if often difficult and problematic relationship between philosophy and a freshly thought-through radical democratic or left-wing politics. In this regard, all of them would recognise the relevance of the carefully phrased sentence with which Bruno Bosteels ends his *Marx and Freud in Latin America*, even if they would probably all have different responses to it: 'The question with which I would like to end, though, is whether we should not also consider the possibility that today, and for the time being, it might be more urgent to liberate us from ethics', because ethics tends to block the use of instincts necessary to achieve radical political change. In his other book, *The Actuality of Communism*, Bosteels, a Belgian political scientist specialising in setting Latin American politics in a global context, offers an introduction in English to the thinking of Álvaro García Linera, to some extent a rival or, better, parallel in Bolivia to the Mujica story in Uruguay. García Linera, like Mujica, had also been a guerrilla fighter in the 1960s and spent time in his country's jails. Because of this experience he has re-emerged into public life in recent times as vice-president to Bolivia's first indigenous national leader, President Evo Morales. However, at this point any comparisons turn into contrasts. García Linera is one more example of a figure well known in Latin American politics since the independence struggles of the early nineteenth century, the intellectual or literary personality with a long trajectory as writer, thinker, journalist and (sometimes) teacher, who feels obliged or is asked to step directly into the political arena. In these respects Mujica is García Linera's exact opposite: an autodidact with, by modern developed world standards, little formal education, who learned to practice political militancy as a way of life almost from childhood but certainly from adolescence, who has never written a book and or in newspapers, and who, first as ex-guerrilla fighter and member of parliament, then as government minister and as national president (now still active senator), has preferred the unprepared, spoken word in speeches, interviews and, while President, weekly radio broadcasts by phone from home or office, to convey his thoughts and feelings on all kinds of issues, general or specific, but always from within the particular context in which he was acting at the time. It is Mujica's acceptance and exploitation of ephemeral, improvised and almost conversational forms as offshoots of his position as permanent militant, with their risks of repetition and self-contradiction, combined with a dependence on others' use of technology to preserve them, that makes Mujica's contribution to left renewal unique. The longer extracts quoted in the last chapter attempt, although of necessity in English translation, to give something of the flavour of Mujica's oral style and skill.

The second important point that Mujica, Derrida and Badiou share is that while all reject the facile and nastily Stalinist notion that present generations must be prepared to accept the demand that they sacrifice everything, including their lives, to contribute toward building a socialist or communist future they know they will not see, all equally accept that what they are voluntarily prepared to dedicate their time, abilities and energy to attempting or outlining now can only be realised, if it is realisable at all, by others in a future they are unlikely to live to see. Indeed, what Mujica calls *socialism*, Badiou *communism* and Derrida *democracy* have in common is that they are always imperfections, never reaching a stage of completion: all of them are always in some essential sense still-to-come. It is this that links Mujica's experience as Uruguayan militant and politician with Badiou's and Derrida's as French full-time philosophers and part-time or occasional activists. All three are equally searchers for alternatives to that lethal, perhaps fatal, globalised combination of neoliberal economics and democratic capitalism. In this context, I would wish to have the dedication of this book to my children seen as symbolic both of this hope for the future and of its diffusion across all continents of the planet, although the pleasure it gives me to do so is real and present.

A final note: I have used only Spanish-language sources related to Mujica himself, it being assumed that interested readers can find access to other relevant material in English themselves. All translations from publications with Spanish titles in the bibliography are my own.

DECEMBER 2015

Acknowledgements

Even a short book written in about nine months from conception to completion generates debts important enough to be recognised at the outset. The first is to Tony Grahame at Sussex Academic who not only accepted the project when it was suggested to him, but then read speedily and carefully the drafts as I sent them, making suggestions that have greatly improved the text. Secondly, I thank José Gabriel Lagos of *Ladiaria* in Montevideo for taking the time to disappear into the archives of its monthly offshoot *Lento* in search of the issue that contained a long interview with José Mujica that I had missed.

Finally, I again have to thank my wife Lilian for putting up with this academic who, supposedly in retirement, spends hours of his waking time reading and writing, and then drops out for much of the rest by watching English and European soccer and BBC period-dress serials on cable TV. Despite this, Lilian still willingly carried out all the negotiations for the rights to use the photographs that feature on the front and back covers, contacting first Alfredo García, director and editor of Montevideo weekly *Voces*, and, through him, the generous and kind photographer himself, Rodrigo López. The front cover photo is from 2009, taken during a photoshoot for a book of interviews that came out during the election campaign that year; it is possible that the photo was taken on the hustings. The back cover photo was taken at Mujica's farm garden in 2013.

I am grateful to all of them – and I am sure José 'Pepe' Mujica will be too. Whether he will feel the same about the rest of the book, which is my responsibility, is another matter.

Either the left decides self-sacrificially to create from below the ideal conditions for an authentic revolution or it reconciles itself to the electoral option and conscientiously revises its strategy.

MARIO BENEDETTI [1963]

The key to understanding the obscure knot between politics, democracy and philosophy thus lies in the fact that the independence of politics creates the place in which the democratic condition of philosophy undergoes a metamorphosis. In this sense, an emancipatory politics contains for philosophy, whether visible or invisible, the watchword that brings about the realization of universality – namely: if all are together, then all are communists! And if all are communists, then all are philosophers!

ALAIN BADIOU [2012]

A real leader is someone who convinces his contemporaries about a move that is way out in front of the hayrick that blocks their view.

JOSÉ 'PEPE' MUJICA [1996]

For many I'm just a bloody lunatic who sometimes has interesting things to say.

JOSÉ 'PEPE' MUJICA [1996]

Those who buy land never lose. There should be socialist revolutions about that.

JOSÉ 'PEPE' MUJICA [1999]

I don't own the left.

JOSÉ 'PEPE' MUJICA [2003]

Introduction

A Portly Knight and His Not So Average First Lady

Look, you're not God, we elected you as something
circumstantial, so don't let it all go to your head.
If you do, you end up with humans divided into categories,
the chosen ones, we begin to have a nobility.
Just now they've begun with the category of
ex-presidents. What sort of organism is that?
They've gone, and goodbye to them. Now
we've begun this category of first lady,
you must be kidding!

JOSÉ 'PEPE' MUJICA [2013]

During the presentation in Montevideo's Town Hall of one of the most recent sources used in the preparation of this book, the well-known Uruguayan historian and political commentator Gerardo Caetano recalled a summary definition of José 'Pepe' Mujica by Daniel Vidart, not only one of Uruguay's most respected social anthropologists but also a long-time friend and political fellow-traveller of ex-President but still Senator Mujica. Vidart had said that Mujica could best be described as a 'Don Quixote with a big dash of Sancho Panza', a reference that, while pleasing Mujica himself, did not only seek to remind us that he was short, sturdy and somewhat fat-bellied rather than lanky and skinny. It also suggested that if he was idealistic to the point at times of becoming hopelessly utopian in his aspirations and expectations of himself, others and the circumstances surrounding them, mixed in with it there was a healthy counterbalance of solid, earthy, pragmatic common sense. In this light, it is hardly surprising to find that during his time as Minister for Agriculture and as President, he was often impatiently lazy on administrative detail, a defect Mujica recognises and one underlined both by the Opposition and by sectors other than his own in The Broad Front, the centre-left coalition he belongs to, including those now in charge of leading this party's third successive five-year period of national government, which took over power from his, the second, on 1 March 2015. While President, however, Mujica had also initiated practical self-help programs to finance worker-generated cooperative enterprises and to construct new homes for slum-dwellers or the homeless that were built by the future owners themselves, rather than being completed and rented out to them at below-market price, with the not infrequent result that they would be ransacked by tenants with no stake in the property's value or future, the bits and pieces winding up as articles for sale at street markets on the city outskirts. While some of these projects have been criticised as unsound investments or for indifferent management, it is also undoubtedly true that some financially unsound businesses have been saved by their former employees and some cooperatively owner-built, moderately or low-priced housing is now available that would not otherwise exist. The following pages will show how loyal Mujica remains to what is a genuinely *sui generis* vision of socialism, but will also demonstrate in what ways and to what extent the Sancho Panza in him controversially enabled him to adapt some parts of it to the deficiencies of a post-dictatorship combination of liberalism and capitalist democracy in the increasingly globalised economy of a small and still developing nation.

Returning to the book presentation mentioned earlier, Caetano added an element apparently missing from the original take on Mujica as a Don Quixote with Sancho Panza overtones when he said that this version of Don Quixote was a 'bad mouth'. It is true that Mujica has a well-recorded tendency to use extremely colourful, rude or crude terms when letting fly at political adversaries (or comrades) who annoy him, and the often highly entertaining gift of saying what he thinks and worrying about any consequences afterwards sometimes got him into infamously international hot water, especially when, as President, it occasionally led him to forget about cameras and open microphones. But there's a Sancho Panza side to this, too. For as much as Mujica likes the Quixotic Sancho version of himself, he sees himself as a 'failed poet' or, more often, as a 'philosopher of the spoken word'. Moreover, a repeated refrain in many of the interviews used as sources for this book is Mujica's lament that modern politics has parted company with philosophy. This will hardly be news to an overseas public entranced by the well-publicised musings on the dangers of unbound consumerism and the consequences for humanity of unchecked climate change at the United Nations or an international environment congress in Rio de Janeiro by an eccentric Uruguayan President who was enough of a people's democrat to insist that a head of state need not dress up to resemble an expensively Italian-suited CEO. Less well known will be how this care for the philosophical base of political thinking goes back not only to the inevitable theoretical underpinnings of the armed struggle and political program of the Tupamaros National Liberation Movement of the 1960s in which Mujica was an early and leading light, but before that to the studies and extracurricular reading he undertook at Preparatory College (a Uruguayan equivalent of Sixth Form or the final two years at high school prior to going on to university) and the courses he audited – Mujica never took a degree – in the Arts Faculty at the Universidad de la República in Montevideo. The most down-to-earth part of the Sancho Panza in this side of Mujica's character is the expression of a personal and political philosophy spiced up with imagery and idioms purloined from the language and context of rural immigrants originally from Spain and Italy. These forebears, who adapted easily to a Uruguayan countryside close to the border with Argentina, taught him much of what still stands him in good stead on the small holding he owns and still works with his wife Lucía Topolansky – also a Broad Front senator – on the outskirts of the capital, not much more than a long stone's throw from where Mujica grew up after his parents moved to Montevideo.

Mujica was not only cavalier with the chores of ministerial and presidential administration. He and his wife were properly libertarian and casual about formalising their relationship. Although together as a couple since they met as fellow Tupamaro guerrilla warriors in the late 1960s – and separated only by the thirteen years spent as political prisoners in the military's jails – Mujica and Topolansky married only in 2005, when Mujica became a minister in the first Broad Front government under Tabaré Vázquez – from whom he would receive the presidential sash in March 2010 and to whom he returned it in March 2015, reportedly with the words 'Keep the seat warm, comrade, because, like you, if my health holds up enough, I'll be back.' However, to see the Mujica and Topolansky marriage as an opportunistic announcement of his political ambitions – the formalisation of their long-haul personal tie was his idea, his wife claims – is unnecessarily hostile. Having chosen the option of continuing their militancy within the Uruguayan democratic system when the thirteen-year dictatorship ended in 1985, both are as committed now to change within this regime as they once were to what they were far from alone in seeing as an imminent chance to overthrow it. That attempt failed, but neither of them has denounced their former commitments nor have they disowned the ideas and vision that underwrote them. The late marriage, seen as a mere legal formality by both the parties involved, can be seen as removing a possible moral barrier that might dissuade some of the voters from other parties that the Broad Front needed to win over and keep. Once again, a pragmatic Sancho Panza defeated the anarchistic inclinations of this Don Quixote.

There is another darker side to the marriage of Mujica and Topolansky that goes deep into what the Broad Front governments have been about, of which the administration under Mujica's tutelage has been to date the most radical example. On 24 April 2014 there took place in the luxurious, fin-de-siècle Hotel del Prado the launching of novelist Pablo Vierci's *The Five of Them* [*ellas 5* in the original Spanish, the *-as* ending indicates that all five referents are female], a recounting through narrative and first-person interview responses of the lives of all five Uruguayan 'first ladies' since the return to democracy in 1985. Of the five, two, Marta Canessa and Mercedes Menafra, are married to the two Colorado party presidents, respectively Julio María Sanguinetti (President twice, 1985–1990 and 1995–2000) and Jorge Batlle (2000–2005), both of them, the second by family connection, closely associated with the Colorado party sector which goes back to the man widely seen as the determining figure in twentieth – century Uruguayan political culture, José Batlle y Ordóñez, whom Mujica nominates as the founder of social democracy in the Western world and not merely of a politics of gradual erosion of class differences and social intolerance that still permeates the Uruguayan national imaginary. Julia Pou is married to the National Party's Luis Alberto Lacalle, who had been President for the period 1990–1995 and would lose to Mujica when he ran for a second term in 2009. The Lacalle family name is as closely aligned to the Nationals as Batlle is the Colorados, and it was Julia and Luis Alberto's son, Luis Lacalle Pou, whom the Broad Front's Tabaré Vázquez would defeat in the 2014 national vote to become only the third man, after Sanguinetti as the second, to be elected as President for a second time (successive presidencies are forbidden by Uruguay's constitution), the first having been the legendary Batlle y Ordóñez mentioned above (for the four-year periods 1903–7 and 1911–15).

However, the democratic liberalism of the early twentieth century had become the economic neo-liberalism of the late twentieth and early twenty-first, a trend slowed by the rejection through plebiscite by the Uruguayan people of the privatisation of some favourite public entities and eventually by a major Argentina-led economic crisis in 2001–2. It was in no small part as a result of these events that Jorge Batlle, grand-nephew of Batlle y Ordóñez, found himself on March 1, 2005, handing over the ribbon of power to Tabaré Vázquez, the first Uruguayan President in many years not to belong to the relatively small number of families associated with one or other of the two historical parties that had between them ruled Uruguay since independence from Spain in 1810, with the Colorados exercising power continuously until 1958, when amid a growing social and economic crisis the Nationalists finally won the chance to effect the first change of government party in Uruguay's history. It is partly due to this background that, María Auxiliadora Delgado, Tabaré Vázquez's wife, a devout Catholic dedicated to un-trumpeted charity and community work under the umbrella of the Church, received the loudest and longest applause of the evening because, having no publicised social or professional life, she was so seldom seen taking the limelight on her own account.

However, these matters came to the forefront when it was the turn of 'first lady' number 5, President Mujica's wife Lucía Topolansky, because she was quite simply not present. Her spot-lit chair in the reserved front row of the very full public seating area was left ostentatiously empty, and no explanation for her absence was offered by any of the three men – none of the female protagonists took the stage – who officially presented the book: its publisher, its author and, once more, the aforementioned historian Gerardo Caetano. Topolansky, of course, was in one crucial way quite different from the other four 'First Ladies': she was not an 'ex' but the current one and, moreover, the leading Senator of the same most voted sector of the Broad Front government party as her husband. Consequently, if a division might be called on an important matter for which the government with only a slim majority could expect no opposition or independent support, disappearing to participate in a largely self-promoting social event was not a viable option. Nevertheless, not even the tersest account of Topolansky's whereabouts was given to the capacity audience that April evening.

Could such an omission be explained by the fact that Topolansky, coming from a well-off middle-class background with an education at a private Catholic girls' school but turning her back on it all by joining the Tupamaro guerrilla movement in the 1960s, might be seen as having betrayed the social class whose interests were best represented by the husbands of the first three ex-First Ladies and their many friends and supporters in the hall of the Hotel del Prado? Does her evident indifference to the expected aesthetics and fashion in dress, accessories and make-up only emphasise how far she has wandered from expected female paths? Any answers would be pure speculation, perhaps, and she has said herself that she enjoyed her meetings with the other women featured in the book, although Mujica is on record as saying he is uncomfortable when he meets former presidents, not because he does not get on with them, but because he is constantly reminded in their presence how different his family, background, loyalties and attitudes are from theirs. It is generally claimed that in Uruguay the political elite has traditionally not been identical with its economic counterpart, however close the links between the two inevitably are in the practice of managing and developing the country. Yet, with each successive Broad Front administration, those links seem to get weaker and further apart, as new political players and entrepreneurs from previously excluded social sectors earn or are offered roles previously taken by members of groups accustomed to decades of old established areas of privilege. This sort of variation in a society's general culture happens slowly and in fits and starts but the beginnings of such change feel palpable in today's Broad Front Uruguay, and many policies of the Mujica presidency served to accelerate the process. What follows has been written in the hope that this pointer toward a route for a genuinely left program within democratic capitalism could be a less obvious but more permanent legacy to the world that indicates how to get beyond our combined obsession with consumption that is driving Mother Nature to the verge of self-destruction. If so, the unusual attractions of a self-managed small farm, a cherished three-legged dog called Manuela (Mujica ran it over with a tractor), a Volkswagen Beetle getting on in years and a short, fat man resembling an Irish leprechaun crossed with a friendly garden gnome who tells us inconvenient truths in words we cannot fail to understand will have served their purpose well.

CHAPTER ONE

MUJICA AS WARRIOR

From Flower Power to Fire Power

*From a flower called Narcissus they extracted two genes they injected
into rice. Result: a miracle called* Golden Rice. *No kidding. We can't
be reactionaries in any area.*

JOSÉ 'PEPE' MUJICA [2009]

Flower Power

At first sight, it might seem trivial or over-clever to associate a term
borrowed from the hippie counterculture of the late 1960s with the
life of a man who was going to follow a trajectory from guerrilla
fighter to national president, and it is certainly true that in the same
period Mujica would have been more likely to be working out how
to steal the soldier's gun and use it on him rather than how to stick
a flower down the barrel while the soldier was still holding it.
However, it is also true that Mujica started growing and selling
flowers before he was ten and, except when in jail, never stopped
doing it until it became too much work for him and his wife toward
the end of his presidency in 2014–15, some seventy odd years later.
Having reverted to being plain Senator Mujica, he still wants to
carry on as an active militant, rejecting a future of just decorating
the House like a useless vase containing no flowers. Moreover, as
boy, adolescent and young man Mujica had to combine study with
work producing and selling the fruits of the land, and it was thanks
to this that the formation of his early political ideas and allegiances
could link the self-reliance of his rural family background of tilling
the earth with the solidarity of family members and neighbours
frequently required to reap a harvest and get it to market and with
the experience of the urban workers who mostly bought what he had
cultivated.

All Uruguayan commentators on Mujica's life and career are
agreed that two factors shaped most if not all the choices he made

as a young man and thereafter. First, his father's untimely death through illness in 1944 when Mujica was only eight years old; secondly, the subsequent importance assumed by his mother and her family (the Cordano Italian connection from a tradition of vine-growing near Genoa) – Cordano would have been Mujica's second surname had he followed tradition and used it – as they occupied the space his receding paternal connections vacated. Indeed, Mujica would only briefly visit the village where his father grew up in the now French-speaking part of the Basque country – Muxica with its original 'x' – while he was President, deferring a return pilgrimage until after he handed over the presidential sash in March 2015.

Mujica's paternal legacy was limited but prophetic. Born on May 20, 1935, Mujica began life at the start of the only dictatorship in Uruguayan political history prior to the brutal military one beginning in June 1973 of which both the antecedents during the previous fifteen years and the consequences from the mid-1980s onwards would be largely responsible for making him the international public figure he has become today. What in Uruguay is known as the 'soft dictatorship' – after the last four letters of the Spanish word 'dictadura' (which mean 'hard') are replaced by the five of 'blanda' (meaning 'soft') to create the invented word 'dictablanda' – began in 1933 when the already democratically elected but conservative, even fascist-friendly President Gabriel Terra in effect staged a non-violent coup against himself. Withdrawing from a cumbersome, collegiate parliament to Montevideo's central fire station, he had himself sworn in again so he could if necessary govern by decree with a new constitution giving him sweeping executive powers he believed necessary to permit him to make rapid decisions amidst the crisis brought on by the stock market crash of 1929. In a gesture not alien to the future Mujica, Socialist Party leader Emilio Frugoni interrupted proceedings with the cry 'Long live Liberty', but the 'soft' label did not prevent this and similar acts of defiance from being ruthlessly suppressed. As the decade progressed, however, an improving economic situation and indications about the real nature of European fascism began to change the minds of some Mussolini, Franco and Hitler sympathisers, a trend amplified by the unfolding of the Second World War, and eventually one of Terra's former political allies gained enough support to stage a successful 'good' countercoup against him in February 1942, with free national elections returning the country to full democracy in November the same year.

Even without the fortuitous dictatorship reference, this political context is relevant in other ways to Mujica because in the late nineteenth century his paternal grandfather, despite having Blanco Party loyalties, had married into the large landowner Terra family, fervent supporters of the Colorado party. Mujica himself would remain loyal to these Blanco ('White') party allegiances passed on from one generation to another as was usual until only very recently, an important point because these markers of political differences between white and red or coloured, found in several South American countries, refer in the Uruguayan case to the two principle sides in the Independence Wars following the defeat of Spanish colonial rule. While the make-up of the two parties became increasingly similar as time went on, the Blanco (now National) party originally favoured a federalist state structure, the rural population of agricultural producers and workers and a more traditional country way of life. The Colorados, on the other hand, advocated a more centralised state with economic and political power based in the port-capital Montevideo, a more urban, cosmopolitan and modern way of living, and the more speculative financial profits that could be derived from the benefits of land and property ownership rather than from what was produced by, in or on them.

Mujica's father inherited land and then went into the concrete block business but he was a victim of the 1930s depression and when he died prematurely in 1941 the family, still living in the semi-rural outskirts of the capital where they had moved before their son's birth, was still suffering the poverty that was the outcome of bankruptcy. It was in this context that Mujica's mother, Lucy Cordano, whom her son remembers always as a strong, resourceful and unsentimental woman, took over the task of providing for the small family (the only other immediate member being Pepe's younger sister). It was typical of Lucy, Mujica has said on several occasions, that when she finally received the widow's pension owed to her some fifteen years after her husband's death, she spent none of the accumulated arrears on herself but bought a bit of extra property she could rent out to help with the family income. Mujica had been around flowers and other land produce for all his childhood but at the ripe old age of seven he was suddenly the man of the house and found himself required to work at it as seriously as he was expected to study at school, a combination not common in the Paso de la Arena of the 1940s, where poverty generally forced families to put children to work fulltime at an early age. Lucy's insistence on making the sacrifices necessary for her son to continue his studies all the way through high school was unusual in the working class culture of the time in Montevideo.

Pepe would help his mother grow and prepare the flowers – usually lilies or gladioli – that she then sold to local florists or took by bus to sell at street markets. The boy grew to love the planting, tending and selling of flowers so that he would go back to it with his wife Lucía – never to be confused with his mother, who had the English name Lucy – when he came out of jail after thirteen years of mostly solitary confinement in subhuman conditions during the military dictatorship. In a hellish time, often his one source of relief and stimulation was the observation of what went on in the earth out of which his many different cells had been crudely dug, while when conditions improved as release time finally approached, a much used chamber pot became an improvised marigold pot – the whole experience 'took me back to my roots', he has wryly joked since. By the 1980s, however, lilies and gladioli had become too much work and he and Lucía erected a set of greenhouses to grow chrysanthemums. One of only two photographs that accompanied him through all his changes of office as deputy, senator, minister and president, shows Lucía surrounded by these flowers in one of several greenhouses built on the small farm they bought in 1985 and where they still live, not far from where he first began to help his mother with her flowers in 1941.

Ironically, one of his mother's customers was Luis Batlle Berres who, following the death of Tomás Berreta would become Colorado President in 1947, having been elected as Vice President the previous year. Nephew to the social democrat reformist president José Batlle y Ordóñez, Batlle Berres would bequeath Mujica some important progressive legislation to be mentioned later, but this more personal contact showed him a way of being a frontline politician -a kind of 'republican simplicity' – that Mujica admired and has never forgotten. Although he lived in an upmarket suburb, Batlle Berres encouraged citizens to talk to him informally about issues that bothered them and often went to his office on the bus, where on occasion he would help Lucy with her flowers. Mujica himself often sold him gladioli that Batlle Berres, a notorious womaniser, would buy for his long-suffering wife on his way home from a tryst. When he was old enough to sell the flowers on his own and bought an old Chevrolet to take them to markets further afield, Mujica would sometimes liberate a few blooms from the President's garden to supplement his own stock. As he jokingly remarks, there was little security in those days! It was now that he got a lot of tips about flower growing from Japanese neighbours and also discovered to his surprise that he sold more flowers in working class street markets than in more fashionable fairs such as Villa Biarritz in the middle class beach suburb of Pocitos (where his future wife Lucía was from originally). Mujica concluded that the working classes had more frequent and closer encounters with death, so visited cemeteries more often. He continued to work on his mother's plot even after setting up his first home with another woman and her child (but not his) when he was eighteen, an economic and emotional arrangement common enough among the poorer working class of the time. As he likes to recall, this was an example of what the title of a famous Uruguayan play calls *Contigo, pan y cebolla*: 'With you it's bread and onions', which may be seen as acceptance, even praise, of the kind of 'dignified poverty' he sees his mother as having provided. However, it also permits a sharper reading: if you only had more ambition and nous, we could live and eat better. Mujica lacked neither, but they would not in his case take the form of merely accepting the way of things but seeking to make more money out of it, though he would continue growing and selling gladioli throughout his years as legal political militant until circumstances obliged him to become a clandestine guerrilla fighter in the late 1960s.

It may have been his mother's flowers that gave Mujica his first taste of the pleasures of getting soil on his hands and of the techniques of growing and selling fresh produce, but still more decisive was the experience provided by her family's success as farmers in the much more conventionally rural setting just outside Carmelo, a town west of Montevideo, near the border with Argentina and, indeed, geographically closer to Buenos Aires than to the Uruguayan capital. From an early age, Pepe was put on a bus to go and spend the summer school holidays with his maternal grandfather Antonio and other nearby family members or friends who also lived off farming or related trades and industries (wine production, for example). As is so frequently the case, it was only much later in his own life that Mujica came to see how much he had learned from him.

Antonio had put together some 400–500 hectares (around 1000 to 1200 acres) of land that he had bought over the years in lots as small as twelve acres. He had come with others in the decade 1870–

1880, bringing all their customs and skills with them from Italy, which enabled them quickly to adapt to a new life produced by the marriage of what the Carmelo environment permitted with a capacity for hard work and a more than basic knowledge of what was involved in working on and living off the land. What perhaps Mujica over the years absorbed most fully was their horizontal and cooperative way of organising themselves, their properties and their work on it. Whether they were growing grapes, tending fruit-trees or harvesting both, a regime of solidarity and reciprocal self-help governed what in effect functioned as a federation of smallholdings. This extended to Lucy on the outskirts of the capital, where her family would regularly receive gifts of produce sent on the bus while Antonio gradually paid off loans or debts that Lucy's often over-stretched income could not cover and, as we have seen, all but took over caring for Mujica during school holidays. It also included a still standing Chapel of Saint Roque built by voluntary contributions of funds and labour.

Antonio was a pragmatic modernist in his view of agriculture. He did not think twice about abandoning old ways that had been clearly surpassed by modern machinery or methods. He grew alfalfa for winter cattle fodder, financed the paving of roads to carry produce, was one of the first in the area to pay to have a telephone line extended from the nearest town and went through three T Ford cars during his short life (he died when only sixty years old). He advocated buying up bits of bare land whenever possible to expand production and provide more work for more people, but had no interest in or much time for urbanised large landholders whose properties produced little or nothing. Antonio's brother, Mujica's great-uncle Juan, was in effect a small private banker for the whole enterprise, while his uncle Ángel, Lucy's brother, a deserter from the Navy – a mess left for Antonio to sort out – was the intellectual of the family, reading voraciously on a wide variety of subjects and always happy to talk deep into the night about any of them.

This experience would be supplemented during Mujica's early and mid adolescence by an interest in cycling. In addition to entering official races with friends, largely for fun, but also to show he could be seriously competitive if he wished, he went off on rides all over the country, sometimes covering several hundred kilometres. This roaming gave him an early insight into the lamentable situation of peasant labourers in rural conditions very much less wholesome and far more unjust than those created on the Cordano family farms. Mujica would have good cause to remember these journeys later.

All of this rubbed off on Mujica in myriad ways. When he and Lucía bought the small farm on which they still live in 1985, they put down two thirds of the modest asking price with their savings, paying off the rest in monthly quotas earned in large part from the chrysanthemums in which they invested before spending money on improving their own living conditions. Mujica at first bought a van to transport the flowers to market, but then realised he was wasting money because the plants did not weigh enough, selling the van and replacing it with a much cheaper 100 cc motor bike and trailer. Over the ensuing thirty years, Mujica and his wife have added to their stock of land, allowing others to live and work on parts of it, and latterly funding and building on it an agricultural college fully integrated into the public Universidad del Trabajo (Work University) system, a Uruguayan equivalent to post-school vocational training institutes. On the other side of things, Mujica has been an avid reader since childhood. He does not have a university degree, but alongside school studies as well as after, he has read widely in history, philosophy, politics and the humanities. In addition, he has become a self-taught specialist in biology, anthropology and ecology (all successors or companions to his reading on flowers) to the extent, while Minister of Agriculture and then President, of driving policies aimed at guiding Uruguay toward becoming an 'agro-intelligent' country along the lines of much more developed Australasian and Scandinavian examples. Moreover, to judge from the hours of dialogue that go into the many book-length interviews that constitute much of the source material for this book, Mujica, like his uncle Ángel, enjoys spending long periods talking through his thoughts and feelings about whatever most preoccupies him about the past, present and future – his own, as well as those of his society and his region, of humanity and the planet. And it is wholly in the spirit that Mujica brings to all matters that if as a child he shared his few toys with children even less well off than he was, he now donates most of the books he buys and reads to local or other public libraries.

As regards his formal education, Mujica finished high school and started but did not complete the years at preparatory college for entry into the University. His late teens were also the start of a life of intense political activism that is still not over, and it was his work in student organisations that led him to audit some classes in the Humanities Faculty at the public Universidad de la República and spend several hours a day reading in the library. It was the most intellectual period of his life, he has said, during which he met friends such as future novelist and political sociologist Alejandro Paternain and the anthropologist-to-be Renzo Pi while attending lectures by exiled Spanish Republic ex-minister José Bergamín and the Uruguayan novelist and Communist Francisco 'Paco' Espínola. With these teachers he read a lot of general Western classic literature as well as Spanish masters such as Cervantes and the 'Golden Age' dramatists, the writers and thinkers of the turn of the twentieth century, foreign historians such as Toynbee as well as Uruguayan history since independence. It was also in the university libraries that he began seriously to read the biology and botany that extended and formalised the knowledge gained from small farming at home and with the Cordano family in Carmelo. All in all, these years between his late teens and early twenties were what Mujica has described as the most intellectually active and adventurous of his life, and formed the foundation of the 'agriculturalist as intellectual' version of himself. He believed his was probably the only home in the largely poor, working-class suburb Paso de la Arena which took regular delivery of both the Socialist Party's daily newspaper *El Sol* [The Sun] and the independent leftist weekly *Marcha*, not only the most important cultural and political publication of its kind in Uruguay from its foundation in 1939 to its closure by the military in 1974 but also one of the pillars in the history of serious Latin American journalism in the twentieth century.

However, perhaps more important were the 'tertulias' or get-togethers Bergamín and Espínola organised for interested students in cafés or at their homes. Not only did the conversations range freely between teachers and students as equals over a whole range of philosophical, political, literary and historical topics (shades of uncle Ángel's after-dinner dialogues), but Mujica became exposed to the important intellectual and literary idiosyncrasies of these two very different writers. From Bergamín, whom Mujica was not alone among Uruguayans in describing as 'one of the most brilliant men I ever met', he would have received his first experience of an intellectual who had both founded an important literary and cultural journal closely associated with the Spanish Republic and had been a member of the centre-left government defeated in the Spanish Civil War. When Mujica and he crossed paths in the early 1950s, however, Bergamín was an example of a phenomenon that would become a commonplace of twentieth century literary and political history across the globe: the errant intellectual/artist as political exile from a home country whose government had threatened or banished him or her. As political refugee in Montevideo between 1947 and 1954 from the right-wing dictatorship of General Francisco Franco, his teaching (Bergamín had insisted that his classes not form part of the formal Faculty curriculum) and writing (especially his essays and journalism) would become exemplary for a whole generation of Uruguayan writers and politicians sympathetic to Bergamín's eclectic mix of Spanish classics, dissident Catholicism and progressive politics. One of his most quoted sentences reads 'To exist is to think and to think is to commit oneself', not only an approach to things likely to meet with Mujica's approval but also one example of an aphoristic and epigrammatic way of polemical thinking (the characteristic manner of Bergamín's prose works) that would rub off on Mujica's own preference for spoken philosophical improvisation, preferably without notes.

The case of Espínola was different but no less instructive in its way. An important local novelist and short story writer on rural themes and of clear Communist allegiance, he took up arms in 1935 as part of a failed insurrection against the Terra dictatorship mentioned above. He taught literary appreciation and history at the University and, together with Bergamín and other earlier teachers at Preparatory College, brought to Mujica a sense of the epic in its different manifestations in the Western tradition from Homer onwards, and in particular a taste for its ironic deflation in Cervantes's *Don Quixote*.

When coming to some provisional conclusions about what Mujica might have derived from this family background and the formal education he received during the period when he was most dependent on the ties and contacts implied in both, it is not necessary to search for some false way of unifying very distinct areas. Nevertheless, it is clear that his experience at home and with the Cordano family showed him a love of the land and a respect for those who worked on and with it, together with the sense that private ownership on a relatively small scale could provide stimulus to expand in such a way as to include more people in the process of increased production and ownership. Completely opposed to the accumulation of unused land by one single individual or enterprise, the Cordanos and their partners in practice functioned as a cooperative in which all who worked also had a financial stake and a responsibility in decisions made on behalf of all. Mujica's experience on the education front in no way conflicted with this. Instead, he received the example of ideologically committed intellectuals and teachers who, although faithful to the demands of the humanistic theories and practices they engaged with, communicated their undoubted expertise without assuming positions of phoney cultural superiority or aloof authority, and who were equally far from the very different perspective of the scientist who dispassionately records the unfolding and results of an experiment that knows no law other than its own. In the evolution of Mujica's ways of doing politics with philosophy we will witness the transformation of many of the elements already existing here in embryonic form.

A Political Apprenticeship

Mujica has remained faithful to a fundamentally Marxist interpretation of history and capitalism ever since he first read him in the University library during 'the most intellectual' period of his life between the unfinished stint at Preparatory College (he was going to study law) and the auditing of lectures at the University. However, he was always critical of the so-called 'existing socialism' of the USSR and its satellites, even before a first visit in 1961, because of the communist bloc's fixed over-bureaucratised methods and the constant surveillance that curtailed individual liberties considered a threat to the State. Indeed, his own personal interpretation of the whole system's collapse in 1989–1990, when nobody and nothing lifted a finger to save it, was that the ruling Communist Party elite had alienated themselves so much from the people they were supposed to be serving, that the latter were prepared to sacrifice even those aspects of the state that favoured them (such as free education and free child and health care, for example) in order to get a root and branch change, whatever the consequences.

Given this, it is quite logical to find that Mujica's ideological allegiance of longest standing has been to anarchism, and he has frequently said over the years that he retains to this day a strongly libertarian bent. If the early anarchist Uruguayan union movement (largely brought by early migrants from Mediterranean countries where the anarchists were strong) failed in the long run, Mujica reminds us that it left behind a culture, a rudimentary but very specific kind of association and the eight-hour working day law.

There is little doubt that the experience of the cooperative organi-zation of his Italian forbears' successful agricultural enterprises down in Carmelo dovetailed neatly into the informal, non-hierar-chic, participatory methods of the anarchist student groups in which he first started his work as political militant while still at high school (unlike many English-speaking countries, student organizations began playing an ever more important role in Uruguay during the crisis decades of the 1950s and 1960s in high school, well before any of the students there became eligible for university). It would be significant in more than just a superficial, cosmetic fashion, and not only for Mujica, that these groups avoided the word 'Party' in their titles, sidestepping from the outset any association with the traditional form of political organization in Uruguay, including Communist and Socialist Parties as well as the two biggest ones that had governed Uruguay since independence. The anarchists Mujica joined as a student, for example, were part of the Uruguayan Anarchist Federation.

However, these paragraphs on Mujica's studies and reading should not lead us to forget that throughout all this time he was also working and entertaining himself. Consequently, just as important, if not more so, than the anarchist groups and the writings of Kropotkin and company, were his friendship and lengthy conver-sations with a newspaper seller in the same market where Mujica sold his flowers. His name was Pedro Boadas and he was a Catalan anarchist trade unionist from Barcelona in exile in Montevideo. He had in the past been caught while attempting to make 'appropria-tions' for the struggle first in Spain, and then in the River Plate region in 1928. He had escaped from prison by tunnel in 1931, an example Mujica would follow some forty years later, after turning out to be only one of many to carry this anarchist strain with him into the functioning of the Tupamaros guerrillas in the 1960s. Indeed, some sources indicate that another exiled Spanish anar-chist, Abraham Guillén, who had also, though twenty years later, made his way to Uruguay via imprisonment in Argentina, produced writings that indicate he was perhaps an inspiration but also a mentor and assessor of Tupamaros urban guerrilla tactics and methods.

While Mujica and his friends were trying out their wings as anar-chist militants, there were changes in mainstream Uruguayan politics that at the time they ignored, criticised or ridiculed. However, there was one reform, initiated by the same President

Batlle Berres who helped Lucy with her flowers on the bus, to whom Mujica himself sold gladioli for his wife and from whose garden he occasionally stole a bloom or two, the importance of which Mujica would later regularly acknowledge, a recognition he would put on the official public record in July 2014 while President himself during the Uruguayan's Senate's homage to Batlle Berres on the fiftieth anniversary of his death in 1964. Batlle Berres had been elected Vice-President in 1946 as the running mate of Tomás Berreta but assumed power in 1947 when Berreta died unexpectedly only five months after beginning his then four-year term (by the early twenty-first century the four years would have been raised to five). Batlle Berres was very much a social reformer, as his already noted taste for informal contact with his electorate suggests, and inherited, as it were, the 'progressive president' mantle once worn by his uncle, José Batlle y Ordoñez, who had earlier in the twentieth century begun the social democratic and liberal legislation that had made Uruguay the first welfare state in the West and remains to this day the strongly influential backdrop to Uruguayan social and political culture. The 1940s and early 1950s saw important changes for wage earners and women as well as the nationalisation of the last British-owned enterprises (tram system, refrigeration and railway network), accompanied by supposedly money-saving and job-creating import-substitution industrialisation policies that reflected the changes imposed on the Uruguayan economy by the end of the Second World War.

It was in this context that parliament finally passed in 1948 some legislation on land reform that had been in the air for twenty years but had been blocked by the influence of large landowners and their representatives. The National Administration Council, empowered by the 1917 constitution, has failed in its attempts to break up these huge estates; the Terra 'benign' dictatorship in the 1930s actively prevented any progress being made on this front, Indeed, it is all but an axiom in Uruguayan social history texts that the impulse for reform witnessed in the first thirty years of the last century effectively stopped at the farm gates in the interior. This may be slightly overstated as a sweeping generalisation, but it remains the case to this day that one of the breaks on Uruguayan development is the large amount of unproductive or under-producing potentially fertile land. A frustrated Mujica has regularly complained that even the Constitution seems to have been written by and for ranchers – his efforts at taxing them, partly to fund improvements to rural public schools, had been declared unconstitutional by the Supreme Court!

These large landowner interests could not prevent the passing of what is called the Colonisation Law in 1948, but they did apparently ensure that resources to implement it were kept to a minimum. Still in force and last amended in 2011 during the Mujica presidency, the legislation was intended to allow the state to purchase unused land and sell or lease it in blocks to smallholders for productive agricultural purposes, in recent times often favouring cooperative ventures that recall that of Mujica's grandfather Antonio from much earlier in the twentieth century. However, although better resourced, even current legislation's impact is still limited by long-standing and powerful conservative interests and instincts. A foreign visitor flying over Uruguay today could be forgiven for seeing the whole country as one large mottled green paddock, but the same visitor travelling overland later would notice how much of that expanse was unused or under utilised in comparison with similar tracts in Europe or the United Kingdom or, to use comparisons that Mujica has always preferred, in Australia or New Zealand.

The next crucial milestone in Mujica's advance towards what would become the Tupamaros guerrilla movement can be summed up with a shorthand reference to a left-wing senator, Enrique Erro, a name that for non-Uruguayans will require more than a little contextualisation. In addition to representing a long-term commitment on Mujica's behalf, as time went by the association with Erro also provided him with legal and political cover for other activities that required protection from public exposure.

In the 1954 elections that brought and end to Batlle Berres's presidency, Mujica, voting for the first time, did so for the Socialist Party of Emilio Frugoni, the same Socialist leader who had interrupted the investiture of Terra as dictator in 1933 with the cry 'Long live Liberty'. It should be noted that the Socialist and Communist parties, both very traditional, perfectly legal organizations of long standing in Uruguay, although very strong in the trade union movement, had in national elections never amassed, even between them, more than about six or seven percent of potential votes across the entire country. This was, in part at least, because they almost ceaselessly squabbled among themselves as well as with other left-wing groups, such as Trotskyists, International Socialists and Anarchists, even less supported by the population at large. These acrimonious disputes over issues major and minor, in addition to the inevitable complaints by others about the futile but destructive disunity of the national Left as a whole, would remain the order of the day until the advent of the Broad Front [Frente Amplio] in 1971.

The Colorado party won the 1954 elections by a fairly comfortable margin but this time the conservative wing effectively put an end to the reformist push led by Batlle Berres by voting in at the same time a return to a collegiate system of government with minority representation by the chief opposition National party that paid lip-service to its post-independence 'Blanco' past but mostly only as juice for its own mythology. This change of government faction coincided with a retraction of the Uruguayan economy following the end of the Korean War in 1953, profits from which conflict had artificially extended a period of relatively easy bonanza that had in turn disguised what was soon revealed as a very retarded and insufficient modernisation of productive processes and infrastructure. The small country was left hopelessly ill prepared to meet the changes in the whole world order that would take place over the next ten to twenty years. Close political and economic alignment with the United States, all but imposed by the exigencies of the Cold War via the newly founded Organisation of American States, would not be an unalloyed benefit, either.

The Uruguayan people's worries and fears about the overall situation were not long in showing themselves in a way dramatic in itself but also a herald of more traumatic events in the not so distant future. In 1958, the National party beat the Colorados in the presidential elections for the first time in ninety-three years. It was the resulting government that would bring Senator Erro to extensive public attention and eventual notoriety for the first time and would expose Mujica, as a trusted friend and member of his staff, to the tough realities and marked limitations of representative democracy Uruguay-style.

Erro and Mujica shared what we have already seen the latter call a 'Blanco' view of history with its preference for its federalist background, its opposition to French and British imperial meddling and its concern for rural workers and others marginalised by the centralised financial capitalism of the port and principal city of Montevideo. They were also alike in revering Aparicio Saravia, leader of the last Blanco insurrection and civil war fought on these grounds, who had been defeated by the forces of Batlle y Ordóñez only as recently as 1904. Mujica had a picture of him in his bedroom when young and it is his legacy and tradition that he and many others still believe to have been betrayed by the party when it had long ago scrapped its 'Blanco' label in favour of the less specifically committed but more inclusive and neutral name of National Party.

These elements of its past and ideology had been kept alive by the National Party's legendary leader Luis Alberto de Herrera, who would die in April 1959 only weeks after his party had finally taken over government of the country. Herrera was an extremely conservative politician – he supported the Terra dictatorship and his sympathies were openly for the Mussolini/Hitler axis during the War – but also a major national historian whose feelings for the rural interior led to strong anti-imperialist sentiments that opposed close alliances with the United States. For Mujica's 'Blanco' reading of Uruguayan history, whereas the National party foreign policy preoccupied itself first with the West and its metropolitan centres of capitalism, Herrera was a nationalist interested in solidarity with the immediate neighbours: he put the nearby region first (the federalist touch), then Latin America and only finally the rest of the world. This Herrera, the 'Blanco'-leaning, traditionalist party-leader and historian, was a friend and regular visitor of the Cordano family down in Carmelo, and it was to a minority sector of the National Party aligned with this 'Blanco' vision of the nation's history that both of Mujica's parents and, later, Enrique Erro associated themselves. Much later, during Mujica's imprisonment under the military dictatorship, his mother Lucy would irrationally maintain that her son was helped by being close to Herrera's tomb despite the cruelty of the conditions in the nearby prison where he was locked up for a few months between the regular transfers.

These were not, however, Mujica's principal allegiances. As he has frequently clarified, he was and remains first and foremost a man of the left and it was to this that he added a dose of 'Blanco' anti-imperialist nationalism. It was in this context that Mujica and Enrique Erro discovered the second point they had in common: a sympathy for workers and their families and a determination to improve their pay packets, their living and working situation and their future prospects. If his background had given Mujica early insight into the plight of peasants and small farmers, it was selling flowers at the street fairs of working class Montevideo suburbs that brought him into contact with the urban workers, especially those in the meat and refrigeration industries. He was never a formal card-carrying member of any trade union, but would show solidarity by working with union or other groups supporting strike and other actions undertaken in the search for better wages and conditions. The men reciprocated by often passing on to the Mujica family some of the meat they received cheaply or free as part of their pay.

In the new National Party government that took office in March 1959, Erro was made Minister of Labour. His very pro-labour approach to the ministry was almost certain to cause problems in an administration that was the result of an election win gained only with the help of a rabidly right-wing, anti-communist, rabble-rousing populist named Benito Nardone. This man, ironically, claimed to represent through a trade union organisation precisely those small scale rural interests and people that so preoccupied Mujica – the latter has even been referred to as a left-wing Nardone in the Uruguayan media. As the economic crisis worsened, Erro's pro-worker line alienated his own party as well as managers and bosses to the extent that he was literally no longer received even by his own government members. Forced to resign, he was replaced by a more docile right-winger, and retreated to work on creating his own sector within the National party, eventually leaving the party altogether to form the Unión Popular [People's Union], an alliance between rene-gade socialists, progressive rural intellectuals and independents that would stand as one of the Socialist options in the 1962 elections.

Mujica accompanied him all through this trajectory, especially in a vibrant, active National party youth movement that Erro started. Here Mujica met future National Party leaders such as Luis Alberto Lacalle who, some fifty years later, would be his rival in the head-to-head run-off for the presidency in 2009, and, more importantly, was able as an official Young Nationals representative to visit the Soviet Union, China and Cuba in the early 1960s. The libertarian in Mujica balked at the vertically rigid bureaucratisation in the Soviet Union and its regimented counterpart in Maoist China and, then as more officially later, argued with members of the Cuban Communist Party and its government over the traces of both in revolutionary Cuba. Nevertheless, like so many budding Latin American revolutionaries of the time, he felt that the hybrid tropi-calised Marxism of the hot and humid Caribbean island was, culturally and ideologically, a more suitable model with which to combat the increasing Coca-colonisation of the Southern Cone of the Americas or of the individual countries within it. This was espe-cially the case for Mujica because his appreciation of rural issues led directly to his admiration for the hard determination of the Cuban 'guajiros', the wiry peasant workers who were the backbone of the

Cuban economy just as they had been central to Fidel Castro and Che Guevara's transformation of a handful of insurgents in 1956 into the revolutionary army that made its triumphant entry into Havana on 1 January 1959. Not surprisingly, perhaps, their Uruguayan counterparts, the rice growers and cane cutters of the hot northern provinces, would play a crucial role in the formation of what would become the Tupamaros guerrilla movement in the mid-1960s.

In the meantime, back in Uruguay things were going from bad to worse. In essence, a decade-old economic model was failing badly but neither the party system nor the collegiate method of government could produce any viable alternatives with enough support to get them going. The result was the growing impoverishment of all, except a more or less corrupt elite at the top, as galloping inflation swallowed up any salary or pension increases and widening social unrest required ever more violent repression to put it down. Until the military brought it to an artificial halt with their coup d'état in June 1973 and attempted to impose an untrammelled liberal economics, this trend would continue and intensify as the 1960s progressed. When the mini-coalition around Erro and the socialists and another led by Communists with the pointed acronym FIDEL failed to attract any appreciable increase in votes for the Left in the 1962 national election, many, including Mujica, quite simply gave up on Uruguayan democracy: 'por acá no va', he reports himself as concluding at the time – 'This way is no way'. Socialism through revolution really seemed 'just around the corner', the title of one of the best books written on the Uruguayan revolutionary left (see Rey Tristán entry in the bibliography).

Fire Power

This not the place for a history of the Tupamaros guerrillas although an account of some fundamental aspects of it is required to make Mujica's role in the movement comprehensible and to establish the foundations of his current way of thinking, of which many of the themes and at least some of the manner have their origins in the collectively attributed – if not always really collectively authored – documents of the Tupamaros National Liberation Movement, hereafter referred to as the MLN after its initials in Spanish. Even in a cursory survey such as this, however, it is only fair to warn the reader about one characteristic common to everything written about the Tupararos, in Spanish or English, at the peak of their activities between 1967 and 1972 or since: no commentator or historian who has written anything at all about this Uruguayan guerrilla movement has proved capable of being entirely dispassionate or wholly even-handed in their treatment of the topic. Of those cited in this book's bibliography, the two that come closest are the aforementioned Eduardo Rey Tristán, perhaps because he is Spanish and considers the Tupamaros in the context of other less well known members of the Uruguayan revolutionary left of the time, and the Frenchman Alain Labrousse in his 2009 history, though not in either version of his 1971 introductory account. The Spanish translation, inciden-tally, was done by Rodolfo Walsh, an Argentine writer later 'disappeared' by the military there for being more than just sympa-thetic to guerrillas fighting in his own country. Fernández Huidobro was a founding member of the Tupamaros and is their de facto offi-cial historian (as well as being, bizarrely and controversially, Minister of Defence in the Mujica administration as well as the current one), while Clara Aldrighi was also an active member and the Gilio volume is an early example of testimonial literature based on interviews with unnamed Uruguayans, both MLN members and ordinary citizens suffering the penury and oppression of the Pacheco government, presented artfully to paint a vivid picture of 1960s Uruguay that all but justifies the MLN's response to it.

On the other side, the Hebert Gatto volume, one of the most cited in later secondary literature on the MLN, is in effect a justification of the existing Uruguayan republic and therefore basically disqual-ifies all the premises on which the Tupamaros based their intervention. Gatto's book has a flattering prologue by an ex-MLN militant, Kimal Amir, whose late abandonment of the movement in Buenos Aires when it seemed pointless to fight on is still seen as treachery by some. The terms of the dismissal of his previous faith and allegiance recall in their virulence – to this writer, at least – the alacrity with which the contributors to Richard Crossman's famous collective volume from the 1950s, *The God That Failed*, vilified the Soviet Union and all their earlier Communist beliefs even more vehemently than they had once defended both. Of the two recent studies in English included, Pablo Brum's, for all its usefully foot-noted scholarship, amounts to an unashamed and, in my view, often naïve justification of American intervention in Uruguayan military and security matters because Brum sees defeating the Tupamaros as having been essential for the survival of Uruguay and the whole region since, though well-intentioned, they were misguided, dangerous and fundamentally wrong. Churchill's book is more straightforward in its approach to the MLN, largely because it is more interested in – and more interesting on – the movement's influence on and connections with contemporary and later radical groups in the United States and elsewhere. As for this book's author, my admiration for Mujica, though qualified at points identified in the text, will be evident on every page, as were the sympathies displayed in two previous books of mine, included in the bibliography here because some of the research for them also fed usefully into this one.

This all but unanimous incapacity to write about the Tupamaros guerrillas without taking sides for or against them, especially among their many Uruguayan commentators, has its motivation in something more general and still ongoing than just the perhaps inevitably strong and deeply held moral feelings aroused by the radical nature of their views and violent actions in the 1960s and 70s, a period now far enough back in history to entail that many of those who study them were not even born at the time of their revolutionary heyday. More important than this, it seems, is the fact that the Tupamaros' beliefs about the Uruguayan state and the form it should take relate directly to issues that are not only as urgent and relevant today as they were forty or fifty years ago. They have, actually, been matters of passionate debate among politicians, intellectuals and the populace at large since Uruguay's independence from Spain and its transformation into a nation and republic in the early nineteenth century. A small wedge or buffer between a much larger Argentina and the giant Brazil, Uruguay, with its almost uniformly arable land, persistently low population (just over three million) and still crucial deep-water harbour, is all but condemned to ask itself anew with each succeeding generation about its viability as a separate entity. Its small size, in every sense, makes Uruguay unavoidably dependent on its neighbours and just as inevitably vulnerable to the influence of dominant foreign powers, whether formally imperialist (Great Britain and France in the past) or not (the United States and, increasingly, China, in the present).

The year 1967, not coincidentally at the start of the MLN's most active few years until 1972, also saw the publication of a book whose title sums up this preoccupation with the very nature and possibility of the nation's existence: *Uruguay as Problem*. It is no surprise to find that the association dedicated to the preservation and propagation of all the works by its author, Alberto Methol Ferré, should have overseen the republication in 2013 of a selection of his essays on South American nation-states and MERCOSUR, the much less successful Southern Cone counterpart based in militarily non-threatening Montevideo to the European Union administered from Brussels, or that a new edition of his emblematically titled 1967 book appeared in 2015, complete with commentaries setting it in a current context. Methol Ferré's overarching theme is that the best hope for a truly viable South America not vulnerable to foreign imperial interests is for the republics to be joined in a federation, second best option to the impossible Simón Bolívar post-independence dream of the entire continent as one federated state divided into semi-autonomous but not separate provinces, rather along the lines of Australia today. This notion dovetails neatly with Mujica's ongoing concern that Uruguay be in effect the agricultural cradle for the continent and his worry that the effects of climate change could wipe out that possibility, while the MLN's fifty year-old hope that some kind of socialist Uruguay might have become the foundation stone of continental federation only underlines the current relevance of historical research into the politics and ideology of the movement.

There is one matter concerning Mujica's involvement with the MLN that requires attention before embarking on an account of it and of those aspects of the movement that proved attractive to him. Mujica is often named as one of the founders of the Tupamaros but this is far from clear, and many of his former brothers in arms emphatically deny it. Since some of these have become political adversaries, especially those who see his later and still current involvement with the trappings of governing a country that persists in remaining a liberal, capitalist democracy as a betrayal of former socialist and revolutionary ideals and aims, they may be seen as having a vested interest in downplaying his role in the movement's early history. However, even allowing for this, there remains more than a little ambiguity surrounding the issue, but it would seem that this has as much to do with the form of Mujica's early involvement as with any perhaps foreseeable wrangling among the movement's participants and historians over responsibility for its creation. While there is no doubt at all about Mujica's involvement in at least some of the actions and discussions by groups with different political backgrounds active in the working class Montevideo districts of La

Teja and Cerro where he largely sold his flowers, he does not seem to have been a protagonist in what was seen by some early in the 1960s as the urgent task of bringing together a single organisation designed to coordinate the activities of such groups.

Rather, it would appear that his libertarian inclinations led Mujica in two opposed directions until later in the MLN's development. He would support and participate in various forms of militancy that promoted the interests and welfare of the working families he came to know and admire or that sought improvement in the wages and conditions of the (mostly) men whose pay packets kept them alive. At the same time, he seems to have avoided anything that would have aligned him too closely with any one of the groups or formal organisations engaged in such activities, preferring to freelance not at whim but rather according to the priorities he perceived different sectors or conjunctures as demanding of him. In other words, Mujica's personal and political commitment at this time was clear but the overall ideology, methodology and purpose that would guide the expressions of this commitment were not fixed. When present at those events or meetings he judged to be valuable, Mujica was a force that could be counted on but as yet its contribution could not be taken for granted by any single organisation. Such preferences would evolve gradually into a permanent tendency to foreground tactics over strategy, not only within the MLN but also after the dictatorship in his activities and decisions as militant, elected representative, minister and president.

The same kind of considerations were not absent from the support we have already seen Mujica giving at this time to the renegade, left-leaning National party senator, then Minister for Labour, Enrique Erro, right up to and beyond his break with the Nationals to form a more socialist Unión Popular. This Socialist party schism, through internal divisions and betrayals, lost them all representation in the parliament at the 1862 elections. Even after coming to the conclusion that 'this way was no way', Mujica retained his personal and political loyalties to Erro and his pro-socialist views on labour and other social questions. However, even though Erro (and his wife) would in the future repay that admiration and friendship with personally risky help for then illegal guerrilla fighters including Mujica, the latter had drawn the line at becoming Senator or Minister Erro's formal secretary with a government position and salary. However useful the money would have been during the years 1959–1962, Mujica would not compromise his beliefs for a reactionary government that oppressed workers, unionists and other left-wing militants while implementing fiercely liberal economic policies demanded by overseas entities such as the International Monetary Fund. If Erro had selected Mujica to go to the Soviet Union, China and Cuba as part of a youth contingent managed by his people, it was out of sympathy with views he thought would be enriched by the experience, not some foolish attempt to buy him off.

The debacle of the 1962 elections is one of the three principal moments Mujica sees as contributing towards the formation of the MLN Tupamaros as a clandestine, armed guerrilla fighting force. He is not alone in believing this and it is important to understand why. The failure of the two coalitions centred around the Communist Party (FIDEL) and the majority sector of the Socialists (of which Erro's was one) convinced many that the traditional Uruguayan left, no matter how repackaged, could make no headway nationally against the long-held and often all but inherited personal or familial loyalties to the two great historical parties, the Colorados and the Nationalists. This was so, in part, because as potential government participants they could offer favours in return for votes, a form of illicit but accepted client-ism that corrupted a supposedly sacred democratic process. What is more, the left was itself partly to blame as it constantly claimed to be seeking unity across the whole centre-left spectrum but the different groups in fact spent most of their time and energy in personal bickering or hair-splitting doctrinal squabbling with rivals who were supposed to be becoming allies. The result was that no real effort was made to come up with anything like a common program that might be addressed to the ninety percent of the electorate that simply didn't even bother to listen to them. Indeed, in a public lecture at the Socialist party headquarters following the 1962 poll, Mario Benedetti, one of the most popular Uruguayan writers of the time and a prominent progressive intellectual with a genuinely wide public to address, told his audience that the left should give up on the whole democratic process. It was, in Benedetti's opinion, so heavily tilted in every possible way against any prospect of real progressive change that participation in it was a distasteful, self-defeating waste of time. Benedetti (for the Senate), like Mujica (for Montevideo's municipal council), had been socialist candidates in the Unión Popular, though both so far down their respective list that even if the combined left doubled its vote they were unlikely to get elected, so there was for both an element of personal disillusion in this defeat of what had been for everyone involved a passionate, political conviction.

It would not be the last time Mujica and Benedetti were political allies. In 1971 Benedetti would co-found and co-lead a radical left movement within the fledgling Broad Front centre-left coalition that would function as a de facto legal front and conduit for the MLN, though it would advocate the possibility of introducing far-reaching reforms via the ballot box rather than the bullet. These last sentences suggest a more positive reading of the Popular Union fiasco: along with FIDEL, its communist-led rival, both attempts at uniting small groups around common ground, although electoral failures in 1962, became important stepping stones toward the founding of the centre-left Broad Front coalition in 1971. The intervening military dictatorship (1973–1985) would prove to have only postponed the continuous electoral rise of this coalition party in post-authoritarian Uruguay to the point of taking power in 2005, a context that would permit the MLN and Mujica to play very different roles than the ones they were preparing for in the 1960s.

The importance of the Uruguayan left's electoral floundering and its accompanying frustrations for understanding how the MLN was to justify its turn from respect for democratic legitimacy to recognition of its legitimate right to violently overthrow it cannot be overstated. The situation gave rise to two parallel and equally powerful convictions: firstly, that the Uruguayan liberal democratic regime effectively disenfranchised all those who felt the need for a radical change in the way the Uruguayan state functioned; secondly, that the state as it currently functioned was primarily responsible for the economic crisis that was impoverishing both the working class as well as an ever-growing proportion of the middle classes, leaving unscathed, at least relatively, an economic elite that supported the governing political elite, where they were not the same groups or families. The result of this was an increasing tendency among a minority of left supporters unconvinced by the rhetorically old-fashioned, too often repeated and consistently failed offerings of the historically well-established Communist and Socialist parties that the pact that tied them to the Uruguayan republic had unravelled to the point of in effect abandoning them to an unacceptable fate. As Mujica has put it: 'What united us at the start was not a shared ideology . . . We were sick to the stomach of a country where only those who could pay could get on. We believed that the *res publica* had a central mission: not to arrange things just for oneself, one's family, friends and fellow party members; it should work for everyone.'

It has since ancient times been an understanding in republics that the people have a right to bring down tyrants by force. This thinking is the source of the justification by Brutus and his fellow conspirators for assassinating Julius Caesar in Shakespeare's play, while its counterrevolutionary reverse will enable Mark Anthony to reimpose the status quo. Such a logic is at the root of the self-justifying and legitimating thought of those who had been persuaded and could persuade others that the state no longer represented or nurtured them in any meaningful way and thereby gave them a right, even a duty, to overthrow it. In the case of Uruguay and other Latin American republics, that notion also lay in the roots of the legitimacy of their decision to liberate themselves from the Spanish monarchy and the remains of its empire early in the nineteenth century. To this day the text of the Verdi-esque operatic Uruguayan national anthem warns 'tyrants' to 'tremble'! It would be convictions of this kind that over the decade from 1963 to 1973 would inspire growing numbers of Uruguayan citizens, especially the young who felt that under the state as it was they had neither political hope nor economically viable future, would rally to the call to bring it down in favour of a totally different and opposed alternative.

It is in this context that it is worth citing an emblematic episode that occurred at Montevideo's Universidad de la República (Uruguay's only public university) in August 1961, amidst growing right-wing hysteria under the conservative National Party government regarding the nefarious influence of communism and the Cuban revolution, especially in student circles. The legendary revolutionary Ernesto 'Che' Guevara, born almost locally in Argentina but by then a minister in the Cuban government, visited Uruguay to take part in an Organisation of American States conference in Punta del Este. During a brief stop in the capital he gave a talk to a crowded hall at the University while thousands waited to get a glimpse of him in the streets outside. In the course of his speech, Guevara told his audience that Uruguayans were lucky in having democratic laws and institutions that guaranteed, among others, their right to speak out and criticise the state. Consequently, he went on, they should exhaust all legal means available to them for making changes before taking up arms as the Cubans had been obliged to do because 'once the first shot has been fired, you can't tell which shot will be the last.' This paragraph is usually quoted by those interested in showing that even Guevara thought the use of violence for political ends was unjustified in Uruguay, implying that the MLN and others who thought otherwise were primarily responsible for provoking the situation that gave rise to the military coup just over a decade later. However, this reading forgets or cunningly omits what Guevara said immediately afterwards: 'For there was no last shot in the Revolution. We had to go on shooting. We were fired at, we had to be hard, we had to execute a few people; we were attacked again, they have gone on attacking us, and they will continue to attack us.' In the almost inevitable disturbances that followed when Guevara left the building, a young schoolteacher and librarian was shot dead. Whether a failed assassination attempt, an ultra-right-wing provocation or a panicking policeman's error, that single shot serves to show how fragile Uruguayans' rights, institutions and laws to which Guevara had referred actually were, even as early as 1961. The MLN and others would indeed take up arms but they were not the first to do so. If the republican pact between state and citizenry had broken down, it was not the MLN that broke it. Not without reason, Carlos Real de Azúa, a political historian fastidious in his accounts of the Uruguayan republic, insisted on calling the Tupamaros not guerrilla fighters but 'political activists with weapons'.

While armed police had been used from the 1950s to put down student or worker riots and demonstrations, the state took a violent turn to the right late in 1967 and for the next five years or so all but waged a brutal if undeclared war on all manifestations of left-wing sympathies and activities, as often as not hardly distinguishing between members of perfectly legal political parties and trade unions and those of clandestine armed urban guerrilla groups, the MLN being by then only the most important of more than a few. With the state doing everything it could – including torture in the jails – to justify the inevitable epithets of 'fascistic', 'tyrannical' and 'dictatorial' that were thrown at it, the 1959 Cuban socialist revolution, in the 1960s at the height of its popularity, looked to many more and more like a viable and desirable alternative national model, even for people with doubts about the role of the Soviet Union and the curtailment of civil liberties within it. As Mujica put it, it was not so much that the Cubans exported the revolution but that an idea of what their version of it could come to be expanded and magnified in the Uruguayan revolutionaries' imagination.

If this first part of Mujica's explanation of the rise of the MLN Tupamaros movement in Uruguay could, with the necessary regional variations, be applied continentally from Nicaragua's Sandinistas or El Salvador's Farabundo Martí Liberation Front in the Central American isthmus all the way south down to Argentina's Montoneros or People's Revolutionary Army, its second element was strictly Uruguayan. Raúl Sendic was a Socialist lawyer who had turned his back on practice in the city and had gone north close to the border with Brazil to offer his services to the rice workers who were, of all those Uruguayan rural labourers whose plight and way of life mattered so much to Mujica, the most underprivileged and exploited. Once there Sendic had helped them organise themselves into a trade union to begin a defence against the near slavery conditions imposed by landowner bosses, and, in the early 1960s, led a mass of them with their families on two legendary marches covering the six hundred odd kilometres all the way to Montevideo. Once there, they could plead their case to politicians and expose the conditions in which they lived and worked to a largely ignorant populace that, inevitably, enjoyed the rice they produced. Their appearance in the capital was a revelation to an urban radical left that, unlike Mujica, had mostly little experience of life and work in the rural interior. What is more, the rice workers exemplified a sector of the population that really needed a much-touted agrarian reform that for many was a mere abstraction or commonplace of revolutionary rhetoric. Meanwhile, the figure of Raúl Sendic himself, an urban professional who had voluntarily dedicated himself to helping the genuinely poor and downtrodden and a socialist intellectual whose actions had a given a new specific meaning to the potential of theory, seemed to many little short of a lay saint, an exemplary figure worthy of emulation.

There were two major consequences to the arrival of Sendic and his rice workers. The first was the creation of a Peasant Support Movement (Movimiento de Apoyo al Campesino – MAC), the third of Mujica's three-pronged account of the MLN's origins. Its purpose was to aid positively in Sendic's plans for the illegal occupation of land as part of his campaign to improve the living conditions of both rice and cane workers and their families in what was for the Montevideo radicals the distant north. The fledgling bunch of near amateurs that would become known as the Tupamaros only three years later carried out its first arms robbery from a shooting range in August 1963. Initiated and planned by Sendic, the raid had been intended to provide arms for the workers to defend themselves when the landowners and the police turned up to evict them after the land appropriations. However, an accident on the road north – the first of many such mishaps in the history of MLN exploits – made all known to the police, and Sendic became not only the leader of the MLN's first illegal action but also the first to have to go underground because he was a wanted man. These acts set the precedent – to be followed by Mujica and hundreds, even thousands, of others – of the total break by a radically different left with the tradition of legality observed by the Socialist and Communist parties in Uruguay since their foundation in 1910 and 1917, respectively.

All this, added to his altruistic work with the rural poor and his role as intellectual creator of the MLN's ideology and methodology and anonymous author of many (though not all) of its principal collectively attributed documents, ensured Sendic's recognition as founder and leader of the MLN, a position acknowledged right up to his relatively early death in 1989 at the age of only sixty-four as a direct result of wounds received in battle prior to his capture in 1972 and of the ill-treatment suffered during his thirteen year imprisonment up to his release with Mujica and seven other MLN 'hostages' in March 1985. A humble ascetic of few words whose near monkish dedication to the cause had consequences for his life as husband and father severe enough to be still unresolved at his death, Sendic lives on as a legendary heroic figure of the left in Latin America as well as in the more concrete form of what he hoped were practical thoughts on a socialist economics for Uruguay and the continent on which he worked in his last years in prison and then published before the onset of his final illness. The influence and importance of these writings remain part of the often acrimonious debate between those who claim to have remained loyal to Sendic's original vision of the MLN and those others – of whom Mujica is currently the most visible example – who claim that Sendic himself was leading the way in the changed conditions of the 1980s towards a position of continuing the struggle within the limitations of the political institutions that twenty years earlier they had all been ready to overthrow.

Mujica's own decision to follow the direct action example led to his first stint in jail in 1964. Caught while attempting to rob a textile factory to raise funds for the cane workers, he spent eight months in a Montevideo jail and unhesitatingly accepted the dishonour of serving time as a common criminal rather than give up his valuable position as a militant able to live openly as a man who lived off growing gladioli for sale in street markets. His comrade in crime on this occasion, a practised 'real' common burglar, managed to escape but himself later became a political prisoner who afterwards fought as a guerrilla in Venezuela and Colombia. For Mujica, this episode demonstrated clearly the dangers of excessive improvisation, though it brought him some useful experience of prison and how to cope with confinement and the varied population cooped up in it. Even more importantly, it gave him his first experience of using jail time for study and intellectual development, an example he would follow whenever he could on subsequent occasions. His readings in biology and biochemistry not only deepened his love of nature and the land – he has described himself as being 'almost pantheistic' with a 'kind of quasi-religious admiration' for the almost unfathomably complex physical and chemical processes that go on in soil and for what grows naturally because of them. The same reading also continued the accumulation of specialised and technical agricultural knowledge begun at the university library and which he would much later bring to his service as Minister and President. When he left prison at the end of his first sentence, he flirted briefly with a group of Communist dissidents but they only confirmed his libertarian preference for less formally organised 'movements' with the more fluid, horizontal, egalitarian, anti-hierarchical mode of functioning he had seen at work in his mother's family cooperatives since boyhood. Mujica would seem to confirm what Regis Debray argues in an essay on the life cycle of socialism: 'Prison was the dissident's second university, his seat of higher learning and greatest moral awareness'.

It was only in 1964 that the Tupamaros finally came into existence as such when an action by MAC and other groups to free three sugarcane workers who had been imprisoned for trying to rob a bank (to get funds for their land appropriation campaign) failed because of a lack of communication between the various parties involved in the release attempt. At the subsequent coordinating committee meeting, the National Liberation Movement emerged, with the additional now internationally recognised sobriquet 'Tupamaros' added on to individualise it. It is important to know that this name refers not so much (if really at all) to the Peruvian Inca insurgent Tupac Amaru (as is still assumed in some texts on the subject) but to characters in a historical novel titled *Ismael* by Uruguayan Eduardo Acevedo Díaz. There, Tupamaros were formally free but exploited peasants who were a mix of ex-slaves, native 'gauchos' or unfortunate 'criollos' (men of Spanish descent born in the colony). These considerations assume importance here because they help to explain Mujica's allegiance to this organisation over any others, legal or clandestine, that might have claimed it. We have already seen his preference for groups that avoided the formal, vertical, top-down chain of command or authority implied by 'party', The words 'national' and 'liberation' captured what were for Mujica and the MLN's founding leadership team the movement's number one priority: a fight for a second national independence, this time from the influence of the United States-led international capitalism and its rich bourgeois allies at home. For Mujica, the MLN and indeed almost the totality of the Uruguayan political and trade union left of the time, this combination distorted the economy while exploiting and oppressing the workers who actually produced the wealth then squandered by the privileged few at home or sent abroad to pay for loans supposedly granted to aid development whose benefits mysteriously never seemed to arrive for those most in need. Finally, the origins of the word 'Tupamaros' emphasise the movement's recognition that the rural poor were even worse off than their counterparts in the city, a perception according perfectly with Mujica's own experience and observations and, it can be added, a view expressed even today in the importance given by all three centre-left administrations since 2005 (not only Mujica's own) to improving the economy and infrastructure of Uruguay's rural interior.

All these considerations feed into the explanation given by Mujica and others – although it is far from unanimous among ex-MLN members – for the Movement's decision to take up arms in the first place. His view has always been that this move was at first fundamentally defensive: first, there was a perceived need, expressed originally by Sendic himself, to have a clandestine armed wing of the left on hand to defend it against any attempt by the right to seek to use the army to impose its will on the whole country; second, following the 1964 military coup in Brazil, the new military regime there made ever more public noises about invading Uruguay if there were ever to be any serious threat of a socialist revolution occurring there, a further stimulus to forming what, in theory at least, might become the basis of a people's army to resist invasion. These concerns predated the ubiquitous references in MLN political documents to Cuban-style socialism, and explain why the only real regret ever expressed by Mujica regarding his and the MLN's political use of armed struggle has been that when the coup was finally staged in June 1973, with the willing compliance of the civilian government, the MLN could not fulfil its original purpose because by then it was a defeated military force and the vast majority of its members were either in jail and torture chamber, or, if they were lucky, in exile.

The years 1965–6 saw the newly named Tupamaros get their first public attention with actions against banks and American firms as representatives of imperialist intentions locally and elsewhere (the Vietnam war, especially). However, accidents and lack of planning and experience brought successful police attention including the first Tupamaro death in action. The result was the formal decision that all those known to the police should become a wholly clandestine army, with only those such as Mujica who was still not identified publically as a member of the Movement staying 'above ground' to be the crucial liaison between the clandestine leadership and the slowly expanding number of adherents still able to remain legal. Mujica's commitment to the MLN was now permanent but only a year later in 1967 would he assume a role really on a par with those much closer to Sendic from the start. In the meantime he could remain openly in contact with his former mentor and friend Senator Erro, for example, without their meetings compromising either of them. Such intermittent though repeated dialogues were only one of several never openly acknowledged interactions between MLN members and legal party politicians.

This moment also saw the opening of a period lasting about three years when the MLN put most of their resources into what they termed 'armed propaganda' exercises, an ideologically better conceptualised extension of their much earlier and amateurish 'Robin Hood' action of distributing free to the poor a load of stolen Xmas trees and other fare, a never repeated gesture which got them noticed but only as misguided criminals with charitable hearts. Now they concentrated on raiding financial institutions and private companies where friendly insiders had given them information revealing the existence of documentation that proved not only corrupt business dealings but confirmed the identity of the people involved as either National or Colorado party politicians or well known members of the economic elite whose families liked to grace the major dailies' social pages. The stolen money increased their military and other resources but more important was the subsequent public humiliation or embarrassment of well-known people of influence and power. This served to confirm the propaganda of many on the left as well as the MLN that the ever increasing sufferings of the working poor and unemployed were in effect paying for the illicit and immoral extravagance of the minority that was selling or throwing the country to the wolves of international finance. The MLN also briefly took over radio stations, interrupting programs to broadcast statements or be their own publicists or embarrassed the army by neutralising the all the occupants of a military barracks while making off with all the weapons in the arsenal. On 8 October 1969, to commemorate the second anniversary of the capture and assassination of Ernesto 'Che' Guevara who had been trying, perhaps foolishly, to initiate a Vietcong-style peasant revolution in the jungles of Bolivia, the Tupamaros briefly took over the whole small country town of Pando not far from the Uruguayan capital – Mujica even wore a tie for one of the few times in his entire life so as to look more like a genuine mourner as the Tupamaros arrived in motor transport disguised as a funeral procession!

The immediate result of these and many other such actions was that the MLN's other task of educating the population at large and winning sympathy for the cause became so enormously successful that floods of disillusioned young people, especially students and budding professionals, all but queued up to work as members or legal supporters. This genuine popularity changed the MLN's nature and its internal functioning: it could divide into units each dedicated to different tasks (military, political, logistical, etc.) while ensuring that each unit maintained a cell structure that limited to a minimum the number of people who knew the identity of other members or details of operations. The MLN could thus widen the scope of what it actually did by having more safe houses, secure escape routes (one of the its engineers made a map of the Montevideo sewer system reputedly more complete and accurate than any drawn up officially, for example), while more groups became capable of working simultaneously but independently of each other. Popularity also brought its disadvantages, however: it became more difficult train new adherents adequately and thereby control all aspects of the organisation and ensure that all units, while at the tactical level working independently on their own initiative, were following the same basic strategic goals and ideological direction worked out through open debate with as wide a contribution by members as possible. More importantly, it became harder to prevent information links and, as the late 1960s turned into the early

1970s, the police and security forces, partly through accumulated experience and partly through foreign training in counterinsurgency measures, were improving their techniques with the inevitable result that they arrested more members and discovered more about the MLN's plans, structure and operational methods. As more people fell to either capture or injuries (sometimes fatal, of course), those who replaced them were inevitably less well trained, less experienced and politically less informed. As the toll on the old guard gradually mounted while the number of actual fighters and supporters increased, the MLN began losing its shape and the capacity for improvised efficiency that had initially made it so effective. It was more vulnerable to discovery, less cohesive, less disciplined, less mobile and, because it was a clandestine organisation, paradoxically less militarily and politically capable than it had been. Mujica himself has said that by the early 1970s the MLN lacked a clear strategy and was consequently relying so much on the pragmatism of mere tactical inventiveness that he found himself repeating an old military adage: If only we had a smaller army!

This summary would be incomplete without some essential historical specifics that give a more concrete sense of what happened on the ground in the period leading up to the military takeover of June 1973. The 1966 elections had seen the Colorados back in power with a more powerful and centralised executive after a constitutional change abolished the collegiate form of government. Vice president Jorge Pacheco Areco took over power shortly afterwards due to the untimely death in office of the mild-mannered if conservative retired general Gestido who had been elected President, and immediately indicated that any solution to the growing political unrest caused by the ongoing economic slide would not be a negotiated one by imposing censorship, de-legalising some left-wing groups and banning some of their media outlets. Governing almost exclusively by repeatedly imposed states of emergency that allowed him to bypass parliament, in September 1971 Pacheco eventually called on the military to take charge of the internal security situation, a change marked by the persecution of not only the guerrillas but also an ever wider spectrum of political or trade union militants engaged in what were still supposed to be perfectly legal activities guaranteed under the Constitution. As one commentator ruefully put it, one measure of Pacheco's period in office was that when he took over in December 1967 the prison system was administered by the Ministry of Education and Culture (suggesting important roles for re-education and rehabilitation) whereas, when he left in March 1972, it was under the Ministry of Defence (emphasising seclusion and punishment, while probably also reflecting the increase in political prisoners detained under the new internal security regime). Mujica has commented laconically that what Uruguay needed at that time was not a strong man but intelligent men.

This change of tactics by the state coupled with the growing success of the security forces' efforts against the Tupamaros transformed the policies practiced by the MLN. Although liaison was maintained between the leaders in prison and the rest of the movement still active in the cities and (to some extent with Raúl Sendic's group) in the interior, there was an increased reliance on military tactics over longer-term political strategies. Although the MLN never used indiscriminate terrorist acts such as bombs in places of public assembly, the kidnapping of foreign 'security advisers', diplomats and bankers and carefully targeted killings of police, security and army officers began to replace the popular 'armed propaganda' operations of the past. This strategic and tactical change resulted in more easily attained propaganda coups for the MLN's enemies and a decline in support for the Tupamaros among the population at large as the number of unintended, supposedly 'innocent' victims went up due to these operations. There also seems little doubt that this militarisation of the MLN's campaign played into the hands of a security service itself now more efficient and better informed.

The MLN never put aside its political work, however. A whole section of the movement had for years been devoted to propaganda work and, as mentioned earlier, in 1971 with the active support of sympathetic independents it founded the '26 of March Independents Movement' that was not only a link between the underground and legalised wing of the Movement. It also became a member of the new centre-left Broad Front coalition, the long sought after united progressive party that included not only Communists and Socialists but other break-away groups from the Colorado, National and Christian Democrat parties. This new venture, which received a grudging one-thumb-up support from an MLN still deeply distrustful of Uruguayan democracy, would make its first public outing in the November 1971 national elections and receive the respectable vote of over eighteen percent of the population, far below the pie-in-the-sky hopes of its early ingenuous supporters but nearly three times better than the divided left's result in any previous ballot. Mujica was one of a majority of MLN's older leaders who supported this exercise, whatever their individual misgivings might be about the Broad Front's chances and limitations, and the MLN declared a unilateral truce for the length of the official election campaign, a decision that perhaps gave decisive room for the State to continue its grim repressive line and prepare itself for a climactic 1972 that would see total military defeat for the MLN.

One of the great ironies of this whole period is that while there were secret and never officially admitted negotiations in army barracks between many Tupamaros leaders (including Mujica and Sendic) and military authorities in the early 1970s, the Pacheco policy of not negotiating officially with the guerrillas might have resulted in the military defeat of the Tupamaros but it also gave the military a winning hand against the State if they wanted to use it. The information obtained though interrogations and captured documents eventually convinced the military that the Uruguayan political and economic elites were as corrupt and incompetent as the MLN and the left had always claimed they were, and became instrumental in the decision adopted by the most reactionary among them to take over all political power themselves, reducing civilians to the level of figureheads (at first) and underlings afterwards. In turn, their own inability to garner sufficient popular support was demonstrated in the resounding 'no' in a 1980 referendum on their attempt to enshrine themselves politically in a new constitution. This unexpected but decisive event heralded the period of gradual opening that would bring an end to the dictatorship in 1984–5.

The MLN was defeated by the armed forces between April and September 1972. Essentially, what seems to have happened is that a younger, more militarist set of leaders had taken over the running of the organisation and in effect tried to beat the enemy at its own game. The previous leadership group was either still in prison or, if among the many who escaped in the early 1970s, were engaged in an unsuccessful attempt to rebuild the MLN from the ground up, often from hideouts in the interior. The resulting dispersal of forces and lack of direction meant that the more complex and long-term possibility of working politically with a now united legal left could not be taken up, while a more cohesive group still based in the capital drastically underestimated the strength and knowledge of the newly reorganised security forces and their unofficial paramilitary allies and went in for what was almost a tit-for-tat battle against them. As more MLN fighters, their safe houses and arms caches were captured, major disagreements over tactics inevitably occurred among the dwindling number of those still free, many of whom fled to Argentina, Chile or Cuba nursing the hope of regrouping and reinventing the Movement from abroad.

Mujica himself was finally forced to go permanently underground in 1969, was seriously wounded twice (on one occasion probably only being saved because the military hospital had been infiltrated by an MLN doctor who was the surgeon on call that night) before being imprisoned and escaping twice. He became a crucial member of the MLN executive committee only in 1972, exactly when the Tupamaros' phase as an active guerrilla force was going into what would be its final crisis, during which Mujica was one of those arrested and tortured, to be kept in captivity until the first democratically elected post-dictatorship government took over in March 1985. As one of the military regime's most important political prisoners, he was moved every so many months to avoid all types of escape plans, since he had participated in earlier spectacularly successful enterprises worthy of British World War Two prisoner-of-war films. Mujica became one of the dictatorship's nine 'hostages', kept as insurance against a resumption of hostilities by any of the regime's many opponents and as leverage in negotiations with other Tupamaros prisoners, among whom there were a small number of important leaders who betrayed many of their formal comrades. The most significant of them, Amodio Pérez, already denounced by some while the MLN was still operative, in August 2015 returned to Uruguay after forty years of exile in Spain (the armed forces' eventually having honoured their pledge of assistance to him and his Tupamara partner Alicia Rey) to launch a book recounting his story as he wants it to be remembered. He gave a forceful if evasive press conference under huge security cover (his ex-comrades' death threat never having been formally rescinded) that doubled as a book launch and media event – organised by the right-wing daily *El País* whose publishing arm also put out the book. In the days that followed, in what were presumably unexpected encounters, Amodio Pérez then faced his accusers among both ex-Tupamaros and retired military officers as witness in a number of court cases concerning still unresolved issues of human rights crimes during the dictatorship. While its author is now under house arrest, Pérez's own book is already not the last on this topic.

Mujica, like many veterans of more conventional wars, is reluctant to talk much about his own personal experiences of the details of combat. However, just as he is known to have been wounded himself on at least two occasions, he has never denied using his own weapons in anger against police and security or military personnel, presumably with at least some success. Rather, he has always admitted full responsibility for his part in what he at the time considered to be a wholly justified course of action. He has never revised that position, preferring to take the same amount of responsibility as he does now now for the different political decisions he makes in the changed conditions of today's Uruguay. Because of this approach to the past and his own participation in it, Mujica bears no ill will towards his opponents. He is known to have visited the policeman who repeatedly shot him at point blank range while he was incapacitated on the ground, talking with him as one old soldier to another, though at the time on different sides of the same conflict. In 1972 Mujica was against vengeance attacks on police or soldiers because of the negative moral affect they had on the populace and the futile political example they presented. These days he talks openly against living with an attitude of vengeance about the losses incurred in a past one is reluctant to let go of, which has occasionally complicated his official relationship with human rights organisations seeking truth and justice for the still 'disappeared' militants (not necessarily MLN members) whose families still do not know their fate or whereabouts. Neither has he entered into details about the torture he endured, wishing to avoid what he has called the 'tortur-ometer' through which there is a kind of unseemly competition about who suffered most. What he has said is that there were moments during his lengthy solitary confinement when he became paranoid to the point of losing his mind and even his military guards accepted that he needed treatment. While he came to the conclusion that the psychiatrist he saw was even more crazy than he was himself, he remains ever grateful to her for getting him permission to read and write, as a result of which he was able again to take up prison studies just as he had a decade earlier while in jail as a supposedly common criminal.

In a strange way, Mujica seems to feel he and his fellow prisoners and 'hostages' were lucky. He heard that an Argentine general, visiting Uruguay after the military coup there as part of the cooperation between the military dictatorships in the Southern Cone, had told his Uruguayan counterparts that the Argentine military would have 'arranged' the deaths of such dangerous subversives and had their corpses dropped in the Atlantic. Mujica puts the difference between the two military regimes down to the ongoing influence of the Uruguayan culture of conviviality among equals promoted by the welfare state mentality of the early twentieth century, an attitude that permeated even the most conservative sections of the armed forces which abruptly ended all negotiations between Tupamaros and generals during 1972 and staged the coup so they could purge the nation of all its harmful and corrupt elements under forcefully but patriotically imposed internal security conditions and in the name of self-proclaimed Catholic family values.

Whatever the motivation for the decision, the MLN leaders were not killed in prison; nor were they driven permanently mad, as one general infamously said in public he hoped they would be. They were allowed to live and, after the military's attempt at proposing their own long-term political alternative was stymied by popular vote in 1980, the closer they got to the date of their eventual release five years later, the less severe became the conditions of their incarceration. They could mix with each other and with other jailed political captives. The result, as Mujica has put it, was that defeat only wiped them out as an armed force but came 'too late to destroy them politically', in part because the years in captivity only added to the already considerable lustre that had accrued to them for having risked life and limb to practise what they preached. They could 'review their history' and prepare themselves for what the MLN might do when they got out. However, none of them imagined how prescient would be the question two of their prison guards were once overheard asking each other: 'How many future ministers have we got in here?' Neither could they have guessed how justified would be the faith that Mujica's mother kept throughout the dictatorship in the even earlier premonition of one her neighbours: 'Mark my words, one day your son will be president.'

CHAPTER TWO

MUJICA AS PHILOSOPHER

It's good to live as one thinks because if you don't,
you may wind up thinking the same way you live.
JOSÉ 'PEPE' MUJICA [2014]

In 2009, Mujica's former Tupamaro comrade and, much later, also
his Minister for Defence, Eleuterio Fernández Huidobro, said that
'Pepe [i.e. Mujica] thinks like Aristotle but talks like Juan Pueblo' '
('John Smith' in English vernacular), while a journalist called him
the 'Plato of the peludos ('poor', referring to those poorest of the
rural poor from the cane and rice plantations in the north of
Uruguay). Mujica's preferred image of himself is that of a writer
who talks instead of putting words on the page (hence the large
number of books devoted to him that are little more than transcrip-
tions of sequences of informal interviews). He sees criticism as a
form of dialogue that is an aid to thinking out loud. Moreover, he
has said repeatedly what he told María Esther Gilio in 2005: 'It's not
possible to do politics without a clear philosophical foundation', an
absence he thought explained much of the 'mediocrity' of modern
politics, while friend and former comrade Daniel Vidart, probably
Uruguay's best known anthropologist, has said that Mujica is quite
simply one of Uruguay's most valuable living intellectuals, which
must be a bit of a surprise to someone with no formal intellectual or
academic qualifications and who did not even finish the Uruguayan
equivalent of Sixth Form or Grade 12. Nevertheless, for Mujica,
'what is not sown in the field of ideas simply won't work', a
metaphor borrowed from his fascination with biology and agriculture and here given wider application.

The insistence on a philosophical base for politics goes at least as
far back as Plato. The intellectual progenitors of the French
Revolution of 1789 were the Enlightenment thinkers and writers
earlier in the century, while the same revolution produced in
Edmund Burke's *Considerations on the French Revolution* one of the
philosophical foundation stones of the English Conservative Party.

And one hardly needs to be a devoted Marxist to have seen quoted Marx's famous statement that philosophers have only interpreted the world while the crucial issue was to change it, Marx himself being a political philosopher and economic historian well before becoming also one of the founders of the first Communist party in 1848 (with just two members, himself and his collaborator, Frederic Engels). Mujica's emphasis on politics' need for philosophical building blocks, therefore, puts him in strong company as inheritor of a tradition of many centuries' standing. This is why this second chapter looks at Mujica as philosopher rather than as politician, and so forms a link between his pre-dictatorship activities as militant or armed warrior and his service as political representative, government minister and finally national president in the next.

In 2009, Mujica thought there was something of a 'crisis is the field of thought', which does not consist of 'going around reading old books. We've already read them . . . It's the panoply of new hypotheses about work, new foundations. We need the audacity the old guys had. We don't just need to go on repeating them. This is a work front; we have no theory. Every theory is provisional, but people need theoretical hypotheses to take steps forward.' Speaking of the Broad Front in particular, he went on: 'We not only demobilised the base, we demobilised intellectual effort! There's nothing more discomforting than intellectuals. And keep in mind that bureaucrats are not intellectuals and neither are specialist technicians in this or that area. No. I respect intellectuals. They are the guys who revise everything, putting forward new adventures in thinking. You have to separate specialist from intellectual. It's in the nature of the intellectual to give birth to things, put forward contradictions, to make people uncomfortable, be a nuisance, always the revisionist and the non-conformist who breaks with patterns. Now, you can't be both the government and that as well; that's why the party has to function well.' Mujica could have been describing two sides of his own character.

Mujica, a Tupamaro Persona?

In 2009 Mujica remembered Raúl Sendic, in many ways the intellectual and political progenitor of the MLN, as saying that every time he founded something, he also created its 'antibody', as though building into it from the outset its own internal contradiction between war and politics, party and movement, separate movement and armed expression of an entire Left threatened by the militarised Right. In Mujica's case, the implication is that the conversion of guerrilla fighter into minister and president is already always implied in the very conception of what the Tupamaros were from their beginnings. But it is also a philosophical statement of principle built into the foundation of a political movement, a combination also very much in the make-up of the now former president.

During the campaign in the second-round run-off vote required in 2009 because neither he nor his Nationalist Party rival and one-time youth movement collaborator Luis Alberto Lacalle had secured more than fifty percent in the first round a month earlier when representatives in both houses of the parliament were elected as well as the President, José Mujica told a packed friendly audience: 'I'll scream it from the rooftops if they like: Out with all –Isms! In with a Left able to think unconventionally! I'm completely done with simplifications . . . I have repented!' No doubt most of his listeners would have understood the perhaps risky reference in the word 'repented' since part of the opposition's scare tactics against Mujica (and others) has consistently been that he has never 'repented' taking up arms against the legitimate government of the 1960s and 1970s. One can probably safely assume his 2009 audience liked the defiance and impudence implied in this, as well as being relieved by the possible implication that his revolutionary ideas of yesteryear were simplifications, whatever they may have thought about the actions inspired by them forty years earlier. However, I suspect few of them – not even Mujica himself, perhaps – could have recalled a supposedly authentic Tupamaro opinion published in the March 3, 1969 issue of a weekly called *Rojo Vivo* [Red Hot] (though not because it was full of Communist or revolutionary propaganda but because it specialised in sensational crime stories apparently based on official police files and reports), in which an unnamed captured Tupamaro fighter offered the following: 'In a word we want the abolition of all property which can be speculated with: absolute equality between the government and those they rule, both in sacrifice and pay. We do not call it an "ism". We are a huge movement whose militants include all sorts of groups from Marxist to Catholic and we do not need an "ism".'

I begin this chapter with an "–Ism" connection – out with abstractions leading only to debate and division; in with actions leading to real change – that crosses the forty years between 1969 and 2009, between revolutionary armed guerrilla war and a run-off election to decide the presidency in what is an extension of the parliamentary and governmental system the earlier war was designed to bring down, since one of its aims is to show to what extent Mujica has been able to either maintain or modify ideas, objectives or programs to which he subscribed in the 1960s. The importance of this is probably self-evident: since Mujica now operates within only a slightly different version of the same legal and political framework he had sought to destroy, in addition to the criticisms from the right, he has inevitably been seen and publicly labelled a traitor and turncoat by former MLN comrades who have felt unable to take the same path. For Mujica, however, this is tantamount to putting up a sign saying 'Closed. Gone Fishing', or worse still, 'Closed. Gone to My Desk to Write Articles for Radical Publications Nobody Reads These Days.' In contrast, Mujica has kept to the radical tactical pragmatism we saw earlier as a not unmitigated blessing in Tupamaro guerrilla practice, which has made it possible for him, and other like-minded former warriors, to adapt their proposals to the demands of a very different political reality and context. Revolution is no longer just round the corner; but reform can be, even radical reform, if one works hard enough at a militancy that is both well thought through and effectively organised. Consequently, we will see several elements from the 1969 statement reappear in modified but still recognisable form in later formulations by Mujica. For example, there is no talk of nationalising or banning all private property, only that which is non-productive or designed to derive profit from speculation. The reference to equality of effort and reward for the governed and those who govern is a reflection of the MLN's incorporation of the egalitarian dream of migrants who arrived off the boats during the nineteenth for whom the nation should be one in which 'naides es más que naides' ['nobody is more than anybody else'], a phrase much quoted by Mujica when justifying his modest way of living while in the highest office in the land. Moreover, the description offered of the motley crew who made up the MLN in 1969 could have been used to describe the centre-left coalition Broad Front for which he was elected President forty years afterwards. The Broad Front, as he has frequently put it, is a 'patch work quilt', but 'how well it shelters us'. As will be shown below, these are far from being the only points of real contact between Mujica's current ideas and those to which he pledged allegiance in the 1960s, but they are enough to show why it was relatively easy for him to make his fine joke about 'repentance'.

Other MLN principles whose long shadow falls across the whole of Mujica's career are found in the (in)famous 'Thirty Questions to a Tupamaro', first published in Chile in 1967, and in effect a literary construction by Raúl Sendic, who created a phoney anonymous interview format to put forward an early formulation of the MLN's political goals and strategies. In the version appended to Alain Labrousse's 1971 translation of his *The Tupamaros*, we read that 'revolutionary situations are created by revolutionary actions' and that 'armed struggle itself hastens the formation of [the] mass movement' guerrilla movements require for success. Ideally, the armed group becomes 'part of the political apparatus of the party of the masses', and the 'task of the left is to unite these people and overcome sectarianism' but unfortunately 'the revolution cannot wait until that day comes.' This in a way takes over from traditional Communist rhetoric about the Party as the vanguard of the people the notion that the actions of a tiny minority can develop the general awareness needed for radical transformation to become a practical possibility.

The danger here is that such an approach turns into mere wilfulness or voluntarism, a messianic belief in one's abilities that leads to the delusion that takes for reality the situation it hopes to bring about. Such error is only encouraged by an overall view of strategy that is 'subject to change if circumstances change' because 'a strategy is developed to respond to a particular situation, and situations change independently of us.' The response to question thirty offers a summary: 'A strategy for revolution depends in part on the conditions we can create by our own efforts, efforts which are part of a total plan leading to the seizure of power, and without losing sight of conditions beyond our control.' It is not difficult to see how such a methodology could give the impression of working well in favourable conditions but that, when the tide turned and the military and political situation favoured the security forces ranged against the MLN, it produced the confusion of tactics with strategy and the excessive reliance on spontaneously creative improvisation that Mujica later condemned as little short of suicidal self-deception. Nevertheless, the drama resulting from the confrontation of political vision with the limitations imposed on both strategy and tactics by the intransigent contingencies of real circumstances will always be a factor in the way Mujica approaches and works through his options as militant in and out of government and in his sector within the coalition of forces that is the Broad Front. Such tensions are perhaps the inevitable result of being an unrepentant socialist who chooses to remain a major player in a system whose dominating coordinates are electoral democracy and globalised capitalism. As he said in 2009, both within the Broad Front and beyond, 'democracy has its rules. For the guy in a hurry who has to get things done, democracy is a nuisance. I'm the first to acknowledge it.'

Other MLN documents (especially those numbered 1 and 5 from 1967 and 1971, respectively) added that the breakdown of the pact between government and the governed expressed itself in the incapacity of the ruling classes to find solutions to the crisis gripping the country and of the existing political parties to govern the country because of their ongoing and worsening 'divisions, internal crises and corruption'. Hence the priority given to national liberation from the grip of these institutions that gave expression to the local political and economic elite (the 'oligarchy') that was the extension of 'imperialist' forces then seen as based mostly in the United States. Another document, 'Some Responses', also from 1971, clarifies that to counter this situation the MLN had evolved from an informal federated organisation in 1964 whose motto was 'Words divide us; actions unite us' into a 'democratic centralism' seven years later in which 'if all that unites us is a theory, it only takes one discrepancy to destroy us', whereas 'when theory is expressed in practice, there arises a new dynamic that brings unity and coherence to the whole.'

The MLN parted company with the advocates of peasant revolution in opting for urban guerrilla struggle – Uruguay having no large jungles or mountainous areas – though their 'Document No. 5' hoped they could count on the 'appalling pay and living conditions of rural workers' to be 'very useful in the struggle in the interior' (a hope not always fulfilled). However, such a national struggle was never envisioned separately from similar ones across the continent – a response to 'Che' Guevara's call for many Vietnams in South America, though what would be missing in this continent was some equivalent to the financial and military aid the anti-American Vietcong forces in the jungle received from powerful foreign allies. The Americans did little or nothing to help the tottering Batista regime in late 1950s Cuba but they would not make that mistake again in the rest of South America in the decades that followed. There would be no major foreign benefactor for the

Tupamaros and revolutionary forces in other Latin American countries – the Soviet Union's cold-war policy of détente looked to placate the United States, not antagonise it and, anyway, South America was too far away to be relevant enough to justify the risk of nuclear war.

Nothing suggests that Mujica has very much altered his negative opinion of international capitalism and of the limitations of electoral democracy or of their combined inability to provide economic and social justice for the impoverished majority of the planet's population. In 2009, he said in interviews published during the election campaign that he could not renounce his faith in socialism and was 'far from being able to swallow the pill of a capitalism' that could be 'gentler'. Not in his opinion: 'capitalism is what it is and that's that. It's built on a conception of the human being as managed, other-directed. It may have been more successful economically' but 'I think humanity has the potential to construct something a bit better. That's what I call socialism with a strong vein of self-management and participation.' Even so, Mujica accepts that the nature, rules and stakes of the local and global political game have changed enough to justify or impose the use of methods and strategies very different from those adopted by the MLN before its military defeat in 1972: 'I need capitalism because I live in it and with it', he said, again in 2009. 'We are struggling in a liberal society where people can vote you in' but can then kick you out if you ask too much of them. Revolution and elections are incompatible, he thought, offering Venezuela as proof.

In this regard, it is worth looking closely at a remarkable speech he made in March 1985 shortly after release from prison, in which we can see the outlines of what would become the MLN's approach to legalised post-dictatorship politics and their connections with the program of its revolutionary past. Mujica typically improvised this speech (he has only exceptionally read word for word previously prepared discourses) but on this occasion did so on the basis of long discussions with other Tupamaro leaders and members, including Raúl Sendic, made possible by the relaxing of confinement conditions during the last weeks of their imprisonment. Delivered under a huge banner that read 'We are a people moving towards national liberation', the resulting bridge between past and future, while elements of its content were a surprise for some, left no doubt of a reconfigured MLN's determination to be a presence in the Uruguayan political restoration for some time to come.

When he emerged from jail with the other Tupamaro 'hostages' in March 1985 the first thing Mujica did was spend a night at his mother's house, reuniting with Lucía only the next day. Almost immediately afterwards the MLN leadership – minus Sendic, who was apparently solving family issues – went into retreat at a Franciscan monastery in the centre of Montevideo to review their situation and decide finally how to go on. As Mujica put it in 2002, the MLN at this stage was little more than an 'emotional patchwork quilt. We'd built up a bit of credit more personal than anything else but that was about it. Everything else was up in the air. It was all far from easy.' Shortly afterwards, anxious sympathisers arranged a public meeting at which Mujica spoke on behalf of the others. His speech comprised a number of elements that were repeated in slightly different ways throughout, the number of reiterations indicating the relative importance, at least in Mujica's version, of each one. By this measure, the main guiding theme was the total erasure of the idea of the MLN as some kind of vanguard leading a huge mass of more or less docile followers. This was replaced by the notion of a participatory form of democracy in which everyone could have a say provided that they did so while adhering to the old Artigas principle that in the new republic nobody should be more equal than anybody else, a dream that seems to have nourished Sendic's more anarchistic vision of a huge popular front, larger than the already existing Broad Front in that, rather than a coalition of groups within a party, it would be a more fluid but integrated movement of freely assembled individuals. So at various points we read the following: 'We are going to go wherever we are invited, without conditions, and we will be there with everyone else and for everyone else . . . Just being up a on a podium doesn't stop you being from below'; 'Already in 1966 we were clear among ourselves that in the ideological struggle no one should insult anyone else, absolutely no one else, and I remind you that passion cannot justify poverty of the soul. We were born to fight for equality and for the dream if not of a new human being, then a somewhat better one' (Mujica's Spanish here deliberately recalled but rejected 'Che' Guevara's concept of the new socialist man); 'Those who fight for equality with too much political power over a handful of people need to be clear that they can't judge the needs of the majority'; 'We are with everyone, for everyone, to show that one can disagree about what is to be done [la práctica/ practice] but still be on the same side . . . I don't accept the way of hatred, not even against those who treated us foully, because hatred is not constructive.'

Mujica offered an example of this compatibility between different individual perspectives on specific issues with collective unified responsibility for and commitment os general plan of action by referring to his 'blanco' reading of national history, his belief that Batlle y Ordóñez's liberal, welfare-state reforms made him the country's most important historical figure after Artigas, within a view, very unusual on the Uruguayan left, that the traditional political parties that had governed since independence were 'not at all worthy only of scorn and derision' and that it was about time the Uruguayan left as a whole started to 'rethink the nation's history and then remake our approach to things': 'I've now been around long enough [Mujica continued, in self-critical mode]to realise that this country's people may have Don Quixote moments but they also have a whole lot of Sancho Panza wisdom.'

The second sacred cow to be slaughtered was the idea of revolution just round the corner, which was replaced by the much more long-term sense of accumulated political experience – achievements and failures – being handed on from generation to generation. 'Leaderships are teams, and a team of leaders will only be successful to the extent that it has been capable of generating better ones. We've got this clear and definite: we are twigs around which the swarm can gather later'; ' . . . being hard on ourselves is the best source of tenderness towards others . . . we can't reach the stars tomorrow, no worthwhile program ever ends, there's no promised land at the end of any program. Or at the end of the second, third, fifth or tenth five-year plan' (readers are reminded that Mujica was saying this five years before the fall of the Berlin wall and the end of so-called 'existing socialism', but then again, neither he nor the MLN had ever thought much of the Soviet Union as a revolutionary example to be emulated). He went on: 'Dreaming does not mean you stop thinking because thinking is how you measure your limitations . . . We need to prepare generation after generation of people to fight to improve the species. But that work never ends. We are brothers to all those in history who have taught us something, that one must do a bit more for others.' Mujica later sums all this up by saying that 'we have to keep diving, sometimes only in the half-light, to dig deep, and there are only two ways of doing this: democracy and science', twin concepts that as freedom and knowledge will accompany him all his life.

After vanguard and imminent revolution, the next formerly solid article of faith to go could hardly be a surprise: guns and the armed struggle, although with a serious proviso. 'We carry on with other weapons our struggle for the same ends . . . If unfortunately, someone tries to rob us of this democratic Spring . . . , then, and only then, will we unfortunately be forced to pick up those other weapons.' There was an awareness throughout Uruguayan society in the early years of the transition out of dictatorship that the nego-tiated democracy was in practice supervised by the military who might, in principle at least, put themselves back in power if they thought the civilian administration was going too far. In such an instance, the Tupamaros were saying, they would do what they had always promised to do in such circumstances, a commitment which only prior defeat had deprived them from fulfilling in June 1973: wage civil war on those staging the coup. In addition, and internal to the MLN, was the fear in some quarters that unilaterally laying down their arms made them very vulnerable to any in the armed forces who, unlike them, had not renounced the ways of hatred and vengeance. This problem of the pros and cons of retaining access to weapons would, as with the IRA in Northern Ireland, dog the political evolution of the MLN for much of the next decade. However, the last lines of the speech would come back to the amnestied and reconstructed MLN's resolution to do what Raúl Sendic called playing the card of democracy 'without aces up our sleeves': 'We are going to be vigilant alongside you, with you, with the whole people, but not at all as avengers with axes in our hands. We are here with you to try to create and construct.'

This was crucial because in Mujica's view of the world nothing is outside the ambit of political struggle: 'I don't believe in any form of human justice. Every kind of justice, in my homespun philos-ophy, is a transaction with the need for vengeance.' To call this 'homespun' is perhaps disingenuous, especially since it is not far from the idea at the root of what is almost a prayer in Jacques Derrida's meditations in *Specters of Marx*: 'If right or law stems from vengeance, as Hamlet seems to complain that it does – before Nietzsche, before Heidegger, before Benjamin – can one not yearn for a justice that one day, a day belonging no longer to history, a quasi-messianic day, would finally be removed from the fatality of vengeance?' It is safe to assume, no doubt, that Mujica does not arrive at his conclusion through such sophisticated philosophical ancestry but also safe to suspect he would not be averse to such utopian hope. It is experience that has given him a rigorously class-based view of matters such as the law and the constitution in which everything that governs, controls and limits what is permissible has been devised to serve the interests of those who themselves almost certainly fought, in parliament or special conventions, over the phrasing and wording of such guiding documents and principles. As nothing stands outside the domain of politics because there is no ground on which to stand that will guarantee objectivity and disinterest, if the majority are to be properly represented in the articles that structure what he state is, they must constantly struggle to build a state that represents them. You do not need to be a Marxist with strong libertarian leanings to believe this; it can be found in the *Communist Manifesto* of 1848 and in the poetry of Bertolt Brecht or, for that matter, albeit sometimes in diluted or implicit form, in the pages of Eric Hobsbawm's historical work and of current issues of the *New Left Review.* In Mujica's case, it explains why for him militancy never ends (it is militants who are forced at some point to stop) and why, at one notorious moment during his presidency, thunderbolts were launched at him from all sides (including his own) when he dared to utter such heresies as 'there are times when politics must take precedence over the law' or 'Uruguay's constitution seems to have been made by and for large landowners.' These remarks might be scandalous to right-wingers who delude themselves into believing that what they say and do is based on universal moral principles, but for Mujica they are all but axiomatic because, in practice, even universal moral principles are already political (as the history of the construction and functioning of any nation's constitution would show the unconvinced, and as Alain Badiou demonstrates in his *Ethics: An Essay on the Understanding of Evil,* the first two chapters of which effectively demolish the conceptualisation and current functioning of the ubiquitous commonplace 'human rights').

Mujica will not always be as careful as he is here in this 1985 speech, which he and his comrades all knew was to be a controversial lynchpin in the building of a new legalised MLN out of the ashes of its defeated clandestine parent, to distinguish between the 'I' that spoke for only himself and that other 'I' that spoke as representative of the current thinking of the movement. (The use of the first person plural 'nosotros'/we is no guide because what the English often term the 'royal we' is a polite commonplace in formal Spanish discourse to refer just to its author). However, readers of this book will immediately see how much of what Mujica said on this occasion dovetails neatly into what we have already gleaned from his personal, familial and political background or, to put it the other way round, how much of that background Mujica found expressed in the Tupamaros' way of thinking about the nation, its history and what was to be done about it. This is important, it seems to me, because it colours the rest of his 'philosophy' to be sampled in the remainder of this chapter as well as his period as president to be covered in the following one. What differentiates Mujica from almost all thinkers and activists on the left – Nelson Mandela, with whom Mujica has occasionally been compared, may be another – is that for him it seems that the word and concept 'I' is, to abuse a phrase, 'always already' permeated through and through with the presence of the 'Other'. Just as, when a child, he spontaneously shared his few toys with kids who had even fewer, and now, as an adult, lives modestly according to his needs, donating up to two thirds of his income to the militant efforts of his sector within the Broad Front coalition or to cooperative construction and education projects, the individual 'Mujica' is, as it were, consistently conceptualised as in solidarity. It is not simply that Mujica is a political animal, but rather that even a libertarian 'I' originates as already collectively politicised, and then lives out a personal ethics predicated on and emanating from it. In this sense, I would say, for Mujica as for few others, politics precedes ethics.

Ever the consistent atheist, Mujica borrows once again from his knowledge of biology and planetary evolution to sum up how he would like things to be after he is gone. 'I don't want to be remembered [he said in 2005]. If I could choose, what I want is to be forgotten. There's nothing worse than nostalgia, than going around believing in dead gods. The thing to do with the dead is to bury them and then respect them once a year on their allotted date . . . Nothing can be built with the dead. People have got to live forwards, audaciously. You've got to serve as fertilizer, not be an obstacle. And to serve as fertilizer means mineralising yourself, simplifying yourself, becoming something useful'. This marries well with Mujica's definition of both the real worth of a political leader and of the only role of love in politics: how well your legacy helps to prepare future generations to carry on the struggle for justice, a struggle which is always already both old and new. It is only at first surprising how well Mujica's whole approach to thinking and doing politics fits perfectly with a typically combative passage from an essay by the

French political philosopher and activist Alain Badiou titled 'The Enigmatic relationship between Philosophy and Politics': 'We could say that what identifies philosophy are not the rules of discourse but the singularity of an act. It is this act that the enemies of Socrates designated as "corrupting youth". "To corrupt youth" is, after all, a very apt name to designate the philosophical act, provided that we understand the meaning of corruption. To corrupt here means to give youth certain means to change their opinion with regard to social norms, to substitute debate and rational critique for imitation and approval, and even, if the question is a matter of principle, to substitute revolt for obedience. But this revolt is neither spontaneous nor aggressive, to the extent that it is the consequence of principles and of a critique offered for the discussion of all.' As we already know, Mujica, like Socrates, prefers to speak his thinking rather than write it, and so would probably not express himself in quite such formal discursive language, but Badiou's idea here becomes even more Mujica-esque when one adds that the book containing this passage is called *Philosophy for Militants*.

When asked in 2005 about the values he esteems most, he answered: 'I think the truth, the value of the truth, the value of a sense of honour, the value of one's word given. I think one's word and a handshake establish a contact as valid as a signed legal contract. I think there are these really old things that have to be brought back to life, rescued and cultivated.' After a brief excursus into the uselessness of a fight against drug abuse that does not begin and end with the culture of the drug consumer, Mujica ends: 'Hence the fundamental value of culture, of systematic proselytising and offering an example oneself. A new society will have to start by changing its culture or it quite simply won't be a new society.' These thoughts may be commonplace but they bear reiteration. Moreover, they aptly express and describe a man who is in many ways, on the one hand, a perpetual student for whom politics and philosophy are inextricably entwined and, at the same time, a perpetual militant for whom political struggle generates the ethics adequate for individuals who live in and with the social structure that struggle produces.

The Left before Taking Power

The paragraphs that follow consist largely of quotations from book length sets of interviews from the years 2002–3, with some additions from others done in the weekly *Búsqueda* [Search] a little earlier. During this time Mujica was first a member of the lower house (from 1994, the first ex-MLN member to be elected to parliament) and then a senator (from 1999). However, the Broad Front centre-left coalition was still in opposition and had never governed at the national level, although it had won the city administration of Montevideo in 1989, the year the legalised MLN was finally allowed to join it, and remains in power there to this day. The Broad Front would finally assume government of the nation in March 2005 in the wake of a massive economic and social crisis of 2001–2 brought about in large part by the total collapse of the Argentine economy. In Uruguay, a cheap seventeen peso dollar that had been used to encourage individuals and companies to take out mortgages and loans in the US currency suddenly more than doubled almost overnight, which bankrupted many families and companies (and led to a flight or withdrawal of dollars that broke smaller private banks) and predictably caused severe unemployment and social unrest. Even some middle-class sectors were reduced virtually to beggary (though less than in neighbouring Argentina). Soup kitchens were set up on street corners literally to keep people alive and international solidarity campaigns were started by Uruguayan expatriates to send money to hungry relatives at home. Though the crisis was not the fault of the Colorado Party government under President Jorge Batlle, some of its reactions to it were questioned and they inevitably paid the price at the next elections on 31 October 2004. However, it should be said that the centre left that took over power in March the following year and benefitted from the recovery that was already under way had only been prevented from winning in 1999 by a constitutional change initiated in 1996 by the two traditional parties that introduced a second round *ballottage* that allowed them to vote together and keep out a Broad Front that had been steadily increasing its share of the vote since 1984. Ironically the Broad Front can be said to have benefitted all round from a constitutional change implemented by its opponents. It meant they avoided being in government during the 2001 crisis, did not require a second round run-off in 2004, winning more than fifty percent of valid votes cast in the first round (Mujica becoming Minister for Agriculture in 2005 under President Tabaré Vázquez), and beating a combined opposition in the *ballottages* of 2009 (when Mujica won against the National Party's Luis Alberto Lacalle) and in 2014 (when Tabaré

Vázquez secured his second presidency against the same party's Luis Lacalle Pou, the older Lacalle's son).

While still in opposition, Mujica's thoughts on matters of politics, capitalism, the left and life affected by all three remain unsullied or uninflected by the exercise of power and the necessity for compromise inevitably entailed in it. They are thus at their purest, most idealistic and least inhibited. Additions, largely from interviews conducted during the election campaigns of 2009 and 2014 and from speeches made during his presidency will show how experience first as minister and then as president modified some initial stances either by qualifying them or strengthening and deepening them in the light of his own and his party's attempts to put them into practice. The overall impression, though, is of a man who finds that being in power does not so much change his ideas as confirm his opinions about the limitations and frustrations regarding the potential of what can be done under the Uruguayan system of democratic government. As he put it a couple of years before the Broad Front got into government: 'Our times [ie. The 1960s and 70s] had the advantage of a light on the horizon so it seemed that change was just round the corner, but it's not like that now. So we need more than ever the lamp of philosophy' to help generate 'intellectual values relatively imaginable, tangible, forward-looking' that can 'mobilise and attract people, something that is there on the horizon that can get you up and moving towards it', a notion expressed differently but more concisely elsewhere: 'People need goals because the cycles of their existence are finite. Society must be made to realise that the horizon is infinite and that there lie all our resources but also our misfortune.' For Mujica, no form of national politics or economics is final; the question is how best to see and understand their imperfections and work out in the specific context in which you find yourself how best to act to promote and bring about improvements. In the early 1960s that had led Mujica and others to the attempt to overthrow violently a state that appeared to them to have welched on the republican deal with its citizens. In the 1980s, after that endeavour had been roundly defeated and its adherents severely punished, the revolutionary option had disappeared. However, for Mujica and many others who would end up in the Broad Front coalition, that would neither vindicate the state the victors had defended nor would it mean that the wish to radically modify it had evaporated. Indeed, one might legitimately wonder, abusing the well-worn phrase from Von Clausewitz that war was the continuation of diplomacy by other means, whether representative democracy was not, at least for Mujica and some others in the Broad Front, the continuation of the revolution by other means as far as conditions would allow.

Mujica seems to have borrowed from those we will see frequently called 'the old anarchists' to underwrite his fundamental view of what the Left is for him and why he believes it deserves his allegiance. The nineteenth century Russian anarchists saw in the survival-of-the-fittest motif in the evolutionary theories of Darwin a reflection of the competitive, cut-throat capitalism of the English Industrial Revolution which surrounded Darwin – and provided him space, time and money – as he wrote up the results of his discoveries on the journeys he had made all over the world. The Russians themselves, however, based on their observations of both *The Origins of Species* and what they saw in the natural world of the frozen North, preferred to emphasise what appeared to them to be cooperation and collaboration among species to ensure survival in harsh conditions. Some of this may well have rubbed off on to Mujica: 'We need a tribe, a "we". There are utopias and there are means towards them. What's in crisis now is more than anything the means; the old utopias remain valid . . . I almost think, though I may be wrong, that what we call socialism is the natural state of functioning for humankind. Socialism is the art of gregariousness. But the gregarious monkey is complex . . . I believe that the development of merchandise and trade and the rest of our civilisation entered into contradiction with the natural way of doing things that had lasted for millennia. We are in conflict with a profound mandate of anthropology, because we are acting against our own real nature.' Mujica repeated much of this in interviews during the election campaign of 2009, while recognising that there could be some 'individualistic, even egotistical, traits' among animals, though still convinced that their instincts for 'cooperation' were clearer. Class analysis gives too much importance to what overlays the basic characteristics of the human being, in his view, and a left politics of the future would need to redress the balance with more anthropology than sociology.

However, whatever its origins and however far back they are, the Left is firmly set in historical time, with its attendant distortions and unpredictability: 'The left is something that belongs to our times. Anyway, I now think that left and right have existed throughout human history, although this terminology may be ours. And this view gives me a perspective I didn't always have on human history, which in my homespun way of thinking is a kind of fidelity to the tools of Marxism. In what sense? That the left is not a post-French Revolution invention but is rather the face of change, constant in humanity, opposite the face of conservatism. The struggle between the two can be seen throughout human history. Maybe one sees only what one wishes to see, but this is how my ideology has developed.' The concept of struggle, with its Darwinist and military associations, remains to this day a constant in all left rhetoric, including Mujica's: 'Even though it seems too theoretical, there is a struggle with immediate effects to rescue values that are in the left's origins. This amounts to a different philosophical position toward being human, and questions what it means to be civilised. It involves immediate issues about levels of participation, decentralisation, the State. This is the antidote to just being in government and exercising power . . . It's crazy to wait until you're in power to discuss these matters', especially, as Mujica has insisted elsewhere, since being in government does not tend to leave you much time or energy for theoretical debate.

Mujica has become highly critical of the idea inherited from Lenin's notion (and Stalin's distortion) of the Communist Party as unquestioned and unquestionable leader of a people whose only job was to follow it and obey it. Mujica realises that this inheritance is expressed by some aspects of the Cuban Revolution which, though severely criticised within the 1960s MLN, still provided much of the socialist blueprint for them: 'I criticise my left for leaving behind common sense, disconnecting from reality, . . . leading to a vanguard approach to things, divorcing itself from the people's presence and participation, converting the task of creating the conditions for transforming society into that of a sect of adepts initiated into the esoteric science of social transformation! In its way, another kind of aristocracy.' The subsequent notion that a present generation may have to be content with permanent sacrifice for a future that may not come and, anyway, they will not see, appears to him to be simply unacceptable: 'It's immoral to tell the unemployed "wait till socialism arrives and it'll fix you up." You can't play with people like that for doctrinal reasons', because 'they need work to live.' Mujica explores this further: 'The left can't go on transmitting this heroic sense of sacrifice in the present to get progress, so that even if we are just dragging ourselves along now, dead tired . . . No, that way doesn't work; it's Stalinist obligation; it has to be something to which people want to devote themselves', and concludes: 'We inherited a [positivist and rationalist idea of the left], to such a degree that sensibility and emotions were just unscientific, a somewhat shameful defect, because they departed from scientific socialism. Later it turned out this was neither very socialist nor very scientific.' Or, in other words, 'We got constipated in a kind of set of determinist prescriptions, that changing who owned the means of production would automatically bring about future stages of social change. But I think the facts proved the opposite: merely changing who owned the means of production didn't necessarily change basic values.' Rather, he said in 2009, while reiterating his belief in socialism as the basis for the only culture that could save humanity from destroying itself, 'the socialist process' should be conceived as the 'parallel, gradual construction, both competitive and emulative', of other ways of 'organising work and society.'

Starting from this position, Mujica opens up the whole Pandora's box of his thoughts on how the Left should act in the present. He is carefully critical of one of Ernesto 'Che' Guevara's most cherished ideas, first put forward in an essay called 'Socialism and the New Man' published in 1965 in the Uruguayan weekly *Marcha*, a beacon for much independent leftist thinking throughout Latin America between its foundation in 1939 and its prohibition by the Uruguayan military in 1974. Mujica comments: '[The New Socialist Man], one of the most beautiful of utopias', begins from the premise that 'a human being to a certain extent makes him – or herself, or rather, can have input into society so that we can improve ourselves. It's got nothing to do with some kind of workshop where we can make people to the taste and pleasure of some vanguard of the proletariat . . . But we are very backward in the task of knowing ourselves, because if we are going to construct a new man, we need first to know the old one, the one who is a result of all that has been lived through up to now. It's curious, but we have studied animals more than ourselves. I would say that the constant improvement of the quality of human beings means incorporating into our whole being, into how we react, into issues involving our daily lives, a whole set of elements that have to do with living together in solidarity.' By the year 2000, the 'new man' would be for Mujica that cross of liberal and libertarian freed from dependency on hierarchical government who could search out solutions and 'put them into practice himself.' However, he also knew that nothing will be achieved 'without very great cultural change. It's too mechanistic to believe that by simply changing property relations human beings will become better people.' The problem is that since the defeats of the 1970s and the collapse of so-called 'existing socialism' around 1990, 'in the field of ideas the left's view of the world is in crisis and it drifts between two positions: either it worships relics from the past and loses touch with present realities, or it abdicates, in fact stops being the left and crosses over to the other side . . . Of course we should worry over the value of the dollar, but if we stick at that the left just becomes, even in the best of cases, a good crisis administrator.'

In our own time, the Left these days needs to be different even if its core values remain what they always have been: 'There are things for which you can forgive the people but which you can't forgive a committed militant of a left-wing group. I can't get angry with a bourgeois who has a Mercedes Benz because he has other values. But we are the incoherent ones when we don't live according to the doctrine we preach. This is a serious problem that comes from forgetting the values of the old anarchists.' Why, Mujica wonders, should socialism automatically involve across the board state ownership of everything: 'The whole question of socialism can be looked at another way. We are all property owners, or should be. These are things that should be up for debate, because how do you actually practice fraternity? What is freedom? In my homespun way of thinking, freedom is that chunk of time when you do what you like, provided it doesn't harm anyone else . . . As a value it's a bit vague, abstract, but it isn't when applied to any one individual. So a society will be more free to the extent that it can guarantee to the people in it that they can do what they like with their bit of time on this planet.' In 2009, he contrasted this with the 'shopping mall civilisation' that all but 'imposed' dictatorially the command to 'buy, buy, buy' whereby 'obligation' eroded any idea of life as 'delight' or 'pleasure'. Only 'philosophical discussion' could convince others of this, however. No 'Pol Pot' style solutions for Mujica, though: the task of 'convincing or persuading others' was 'part of being free.' Hence his repeated preference for 'privately owned, group-run cooperatives', with 'workshops', if necessary, to teach people how to make 'self-management' work and his praise for what he saw as 'younger, multi-tasked entrepreneurs' because 'private initiative that explodes into small solutions can save you a load of headaches and is more a solution than a problem.' For Mujica small business is a better response to the need for job creation than the big, multinational corporations can offer, however necessary the latter may be in massively expensive enterprises such as mining and oil production.

However, for Mujica that does not automatically involve a complacent capitulation to the attractions of liberal democracy. Indeed, he castigates the ex-sixties left that has 're-evaluated the role of liberal democracy now has a somatic consubstantiation with that liberal democracy . . . But the sad thing is not the position in itself, which is understandable enough, but rather that they give off the image of a history of democracy that has reached the final step . . . , that the liberal democracy we know is the sum total of our civilisation, that we have no need to ask for more. But part of the essence of democracy is that of never seeing itself as finished or perfect. Seen like that politics has no subject . . . it's like the end of history.' Mujica may reach back to the origins of anarchism but here he is at one with some of his contemporaries. Jacques Derrida's *Politics of Friendship* points repeatedly to a form of democracy that is still to come while his *Specters of Marx* eloquently and cogently lambasts the self-satisfied triumphalism of the combination of global neoliberal economics and the highly conservative democracy of Reagan and Thatcher at the time of the collapse of the Soviet Union and its satellites as found in Fukuyama's *The End of History and the Last Man*, as indeed does the central chapter of Badiou's *Of an Obscure Disaster*, which ends by suggesting that if the implications of arguments such as Fukuyama's are taken seriously, then the only conclusion is that what Badiou pejoratively calls 'capital-parliamentarianism' would become the 'political definition of the whole of humanity', 'commensurate with the very Idea of humanity', but that 'this is, precisely, what the philosopher cannot accept'. Neither can Mujica, either as philosopher or as militant, since he conceives the Left's task in our current context in a similar way: 'I conceive the revolution like that, as a stairway one climbs step by step, and not as one huge effort which gets you to the top so you can say "we've arrived". We never arrive.' Once again, Derrida's Marxian specters would appear to be haunting Mujica: 'communism has always been and will remain spectral: it is always still to come and is distinguished, like democracy itself, for every living present understood as plenitude of a presence-to-itself . . . . Capitalist societies can always heave a sigh of relief and say to themselves: communism is finished since the collapse of the totalitarianisms of the twentieth century and not only is it finished, but it did not take place, it was only a ghost. They do no more than disavow the undeniable itself: a ghost never dies, it remains always to come and [make a] comeback.'

But of course, as Marx and Freud have taught us, what returns or comes back seldom if ever does so in a form that is either immediately recognisable or easily understood. In other words, what may end as a step toward socialism may not appear as such to its protagonists. Badiou once again: '[With the end of Soviet communism], in countries of both East and West, the history of politics is only beginning, has scarcely begun. The ruin of the identification of the State with the Truth inaugurates this beginning. Everything is still to be invented.' Considerations such as these allow Mujica to continue as follows at the point where I had Derrida interrupt him: 'For now, the most important thing is for the Broad Front to get into government, not for us, but for the Uruguayan people. The Front will serve as a cause, a utopia without a finishing date, but it will have an important cushioning effect, through its own weight . . . But among us there will appear the same contradictions as in the rest of society. But in any case, if a better left is needed, it will only be after people have saluted the failure or success of this one. David always finds a way to fight with Goliath . . . A final program? To give birth to another civilisation, because if we adapt to this one we'll have stopped being the Left.' In the meantime, the left must learn how to govern, and for Mujica this involves being hard on corruption, offering the example of a full-on commitment at the top so it stands a better chance of being reciprocated from below and can solve the most dramatic problems, beginning with unemployment and lack of food. In doing this, there are a couple of guiding principles Mujica wishes to be kept in mind, both of which in the form of assessing and approving budget priorities lead to fierce internal debate within the Broad Front coalition because of the inevitable gap between the approaches to society and economy by the centre and the left. First, 'the idea of solidarity and income redistribution cannot [be allowed to] result in economic paralysis', while even before enunciating any project, it seems wise to remember that any 'proposed project is always a commitment because it involves budgeting for what it will be and sorting through what attitude to take toward what it will be.'

Utopian optimism is the fuel of commitment: 'Real problems [he tells us all] cannot be allowed to make us feel condemned to total negativity. We might have felt like that when we were in prison with no end in sight but we didn't see it like that then and it gradually became clear it was not the end of history. The old turn of the century anarchists fighting for an 8-hour working day, did they have any reason to be optimists? No. The optimism was all in their heads.' Such heady illusions must, however, be tempered by a pragmatic and ruthlessly honest assessment of what the realities of the national situation are, that frames Mujica's outline for a left economics. 'There are questions of dignity. We can't have a society in which pets are better cared for than many people.' It is this belief that leads towards what the priorities of economic policy should be for a government that earns the right to see itself as of the left. A caricature of the United States makes the point: 'Even in North America the low figures for unemployment are obtained by increasing the number of working poor on wages that are pathetic for that type of society. The concentration of wealth produces the type of gentleman who has several drivers, several gardeners, several butlers, the lady who takes the kids to school . . . there's no growth in other kinds of work [for the poor].' This of course is manifestly untrue if taken literally, but Mujica's point is that the American liberal dream is necessarily built on exclusions. Some can exploit the system successfully but they and those already at the top require a pool of available cheap labour to make their ascent possible and secure, thus ensuring that inequality becomes and remains a requirement of the entire structure of the ostensibly rich liberal edifice. Mujica can now go on to argue that 'unemployment is the objective tendency toward the marginalization of parts of humanity. Even a developing society tends to leave a number of people cast off like rubbish dump dogs . . . quite simply, the modern city can't provide halfway decent answers for a whole lot of poor people. I think there can be more dignified forms of getting along through the organizing of human beings to struggle collectively against poverty.' This last sentence rings with echoes of the rural cooperatives we have already seen to be so attractive to Mujica since childhood, but even leaving that aside (it will re-emerge later), it is clear that for him, especially in 2002–3 as Uruguay was still in the grip of the economic crisis that had climaxed a year earlier, a war on poverty through the creation of worthwhile employment was the first priority of any incoming progressive government: 'A left-wing program should take as its grand purpose the promotion and incorporation of the poor. Because we can't integrate with anybody if we can't integrate with ourselves first; the opposite is crazy, it would create two humanities.' A spin-off from this approach to poverty is his view of retirement: 'We need to rethink the idea of the pensioner, get rid of the notion of the closed file, that we reach the stage of inactivity', a trait that at the age of eighty can hardly be attributed to him.

For Mujica, by 2002 the neoliberalism applied across the board by President Carlos Menem in Argentina had gone too far, resulting in the crisis that overflowed into neighbouring Uruguay, whose Colorado and National party governments were largely following the same move toward privatisation of state agencies and the lifting of all restrictions on the indiscriminate and arbitrary (and unelected) dictates of market forces. Mass mobilisation by the Uruguayan left in the 1990s had halted this process through plebiscites against the privatisation of state assets. Even so, Mujica was convinced that even the agencies of international finance capitalism such as the World Bank and International Monetary Fund would conclude that some kind of neokeynesianism would be needed to start turning the marginalised into small scale consumers because 'the first answer for those who are really screwed is for them to eat better.' The English economist John Maynard Keynes had famously argued successfully early in the twentieth century that debt-financed investment by the state in large-scale renewal of infrastructure could kick-start an economy out of depression, creating over time the wealth required not only to repay the debt but also to bring the internal market to self-sustaining health, the ensuing worker prosperity not coincidentally ensuring there would be no repetition on English soil of a Russian style post-war revolution against capitalism. The tussle between the relative merits of private ownership and entrepreneurial initiative against state-controlled projects and enterprises would be a constant of all three Broad Front administrations in Uruguay, from the first in 2005 up to the time of writing (mid to late 2015). Mujica's view on this matter is quite straightforward: just because some state enterprises are not financially viable doesn't mean you should 'destroy the whole scaffolding. Handing everything over to private industry simply makes you a capitalist. The best way to defend the State is to take its veil off, so people can say as they do in Scandinavia, yes, I pay taxes but I can see what they are used for.' So Mujica defends monopoly state agencies for essential services because deregulation in the name of free trade practices simply leaves you at the mercy of 'a handful of multinationals.' 'Competition is one thing [he said in 2009], but being taken for a mug is something else.'

From this view of the active role of the state in Uruguay's version of capitalist democracy comes Mujica's conviction that learning how to manage bankruptcy or default, cancelling chunks of public debt, which 'although it sounds crazy, can't be discounted because it may be a sign of the times. The other choice, cut back and pay up, running the risk of brutal internal crisis through even greater austerity, which society might not be able to tolerate . . . The old left "I won't pay" must be translated today into "I'm going to pay but I'm broke". It's a difference in tone.' Moreover, 'Uruguay's crisis can be backed financially, even by one of our neighbours. Hence the importance for us of ties with the region', a position maintained by all the Broad Front administrations, despite the self-evident deficiencies of continental organisations such as MERCOSUR and UNASUR, which tend to leave Uruguay and other small nations at the mercy of the bigger players or to become prisoners of their own bureaucratic complexity. If all other options fail and 'there's to be fiscal readjustment, it must be borne by those who can cope with it and not allowed to be dumped by market forces on the shoulders of social sectors already too poor to cope', an argument that would come to the fore in the Uruguayan union movement when the period of rapid and good economic growth that had favoured the first two Broad Front governments all but came to a grinding halt during the early months of the third because of the contraction in some of the strongest of Uruguay's trading partners (China, Brazil and Argentina, as well as in Europe).

The crisis in the first years of the new millennium only reinforced views Mujica had held since the 1960s. For him, globalisation involves about 20% of humanity; 'the rest are like sub-humans, somewhere between monkey and man.' In other words, it all depends whether you are among the minority of globalisers or rather end up amidst the vast numbers of the globalised: 'The worst thing' is that 'rich countries export to us their values, their way of doing things, their customs, but not their resources', so a globalised market 'must tend toward mediocrity because it seeks to standardize everything; respect for other cultures is against economic efficiency because you have to work at the artisan's scale.' As a result, 'we still need to rediscover the country in many ways because our governing classes remain prisoners of financial capital, a dream that is invoiced far away.' And there's a need to fortify national central banks so as to avoid the need to appeal to international organisations like the IMF, for even 'those many who criticise the excesses of consumerism are nonetheless its victims.' 'The State is currently a block on the freedom of multinational companies but, and I say this as a protectionist, I believe a crisis of the nation state to be inevitable . . . The global market will eventually break down all frontiers, making decentralisation a necessity.'

Against all this, one has to face ones own limitations and learn to live with them by making use of them. Uruguay is a 'frontier country.' It can't do 'gigantic exports', but can do 'a lot of 5-kilo parcels'. It therefore needs to learn how to make this option attractive to others. 'When one's country is small, independence is achieved through multiple interdependencies', in which context he tells us that New Zealand, a country Mujica frequently compares to Uruguay, exports to 117 different countries. 'Those who sell their work badly will not do well however well they work', so Uruguay should look to examples of other small countries (here he names Norway, Switzerland) and find out where they stand in relation to the big centres and blocks, important because the loss of industrial jobs can never be replaced by more primary product exports: 'You go backwards developmentally.'

These specific comments on certain aspects of the left's perhaps necessary passage through capitalism have for Mujica an underlay: 'I am more convinced with every day that passes that socialism cannot be constructed in a poor country . . . Each day I'm a bit closer to Marx and a bit further from Lenin', Marx having maintained that socialism would come out of the implosion of capitalism once it reached a certain critical stage that so far in practice has never been attained, while Lenin believed that socialism could be built out of the ruins of Tsarist Russia after the first world war. Mujica explains further: 'I don't think socialism can be the child of poverty. For me poverty and misery are just that, poverty and misery, they don't generate anything. Which doesn't mean that relative wealth, relatively good labour relations, a society getting richer, will necessarily lead toward socialism. No! But between two roads neither of which necessarily gets to socialism I prefer the social democratic one!' However, he then links social democracy to a libertarian critique of liberalism: 'Social democracy is the mature fruit of an almost post-industrial society in places where there exist already incorporated workers' rights and gains, the presence of the state in the solution to multiple problems, all of which gives society a tone a million miles from the prevailing conditions in Africa or South America . . . We've seen profound attempts at it, like [Olof] Palme's, who criticised

Communist Party communism as the longest road to capitalism and said [social democrats like himself] will get to socialism first. They took him out, assassinating him in cowardly fashion . . . But in the end, social democracy just makes capitalism easier to bear and stays within the frame of liberal democracy – which is no small thing necessarily, of course! . . . Among the many criticisms that can be made of liberalism the most important is how little liberal it really is. One should not criticise it for being liberal but for lying! The only thing it really respects is the surface of capitalism, which it scratches a bit with some redistribution while carrying on the appropriation of the workers' surplus value. After that, it's just a philosophy and a worldview. There may be in the future a deeper, more progressive form of liberalism, but it's not in this bland ordinary liberalism they try to sell us.'

For Mujica, 'liberty is being able to do what you want with your own time. Working less to be able to have more time to just live. But that implies being spare in our consumption, stopping indebting ourselves to stay on the train that marks our civilisation, because then you have to work double just to pay the debts, and so it goes on till tomb's day ['hasta la tumba' in Spanish]! Where's the sense in it? And they call it a quality life!' And again, 'he who thinks that happiness is accumulating money and things can go screw himself. I don't want to make an apology for poverty but one needs to wonder whether it's worth enslaving oneself working to be a consumer, not seeing that you're paying for it with your life'. Against all this he affirms his libertarianism: 'I pursue the libertarian utopia. I don't think capitalist society will ever be really liberal. By definition. Because the concentration of economic power inhibits any liberal development . . . The old anarchism is the most far-reaching form of liberalism, an ultraliberal utopia. In the Marxist utopian sense of a state that withers away and a world without classes. The renunciation of any kind of coercion . . . That's it there! But it's all too serious a business to be left to a bunch of fraudulent econometricians!'

Horizontal and Egalitarian or Vertical and Hierarchical?

The Batlle y Ordoñez early twentieth century welfare state model left a culture – some would call it a sick hangover – that promised or attempted to provide for its citizens a dignified way of life literally from the cradle to the grave. In this still active Uruguayan mindset, the purpose of the State is to provide people and families with jobs and all you need to live, instead of being there to actually help others to do productive activities. There has for decades existed a culture of public employment rather than of public service which is only now beginning to change, although not consistently and not across the board. There is, then, a general view in Uruguay that public servants are not in their offices or at their counters to work but to ensure that at last some citizens can avoid the dole queue and get a pension at the end of a limited and unadventurous life on low to moderate pay. Nationalist president Luis Lacalle once infamously said of his public servants that they pretended to work and he pretended to pay them, an opinion for which he was, not unexpectedly, much criticised. The central question is not how true this statement was, however, but how well it encapsulates a mentality to which many, even most, contemporary Uruguayans are willing to conform. Its downside is a distrust or envy of excellence (except in sport, perhaps) since in a republic in which no-one is supposedly better than anyone else, acquiring more than most becomes suspicious even if others might really want more than a bit of it! As the aforementioned writer Mario Benedetti once remarked as far back as 1970, when Mujica was still fighting his guerrilla war, Uruguay was a small country that seemed made for socialism. However, even under capitalism, there remains the very real issue that in a country of only three million or so inhabitants the State is almost inevitably going to be the biggest employer because there are simply not enough customers of any kind to support large numbers of private businesses of all sorts and sizes, unless they are at least partially and successfully export-oriented. These are complex matters involving nebulous concepts like 'national character' and consensus about them is either unlikely or impossible, yet what is undoubtedly true is that there exists a whole library of Uruguayan books and films about them and that most Uruguayans, when prodded, seem to have lengthy, loud, more or less informed opinions about any or all of them.

Enough has been said on all this already in one way or another to know where Mujica stands in principle with regard to it. He favours the kind of social organisation that allows the fullest participation of the largest proportion possible in making the decisions that affect them all. His preference for cooperative enterprises is well known because he believes that people give their best when they have a material and moral stake in what they are required to work at. For Mujica, commitment, effort and satisfaction increase in proportion to the responsibility everyone feels for both the gains brought by success as well as the setbacks suffered due to mistakes or short-sighted planning. However, before becoming either minister or president, and even more afterwards, he was aware that governing a country such as Uruguay could not be done in the same way you might run a farming co-op of only twenty families, say. Even so, his views demonstrate quite clearly the personal and political drama of balancing his anarchistic predilection for the unregulated participation of all with a realistic assessment of what is needed to administer a nation with the history and system of government the current state of Uruguay has inherited.

'The people on the street [he said in 2002] have a brilliantly rational Sancho Panza way of thinking. Or we understand and love them the way they are, or we'll end up with a voluntarist revolution run by a handful of pissed-off intellectuals that is neither participatory nor democratic. I know it's open to a lot of debate because Sancho at times is Don Quixote but at others you can't ask him to live Don Quixote's life . . . Don Quixote without Sancho cannot exist, they need one another . . . People need material stimuli, but they must also feel the satisfaction of having worked for them and thereby of deserving them. Handouts do not work.' The coupling of Don Quixote and Sancho Panza borrowed from Cervantes's novel is a favourite with Mujica, perhaps because he cuts such a Sancho Panza figure himself (in Spanish, 'panza' is belly) and, as in this passage, frequently tempers his own utopian idealism, which may be at risk of self-delusion quite as much as that of the knight who can mistake windmills for giants or flocks of sheep for massed armies, with a good dose of down-to-earth, plain sense. Here Mujica reminds himself as much as anyone else that it is the man and woman in the street a left government must work with, not some artificially invented ideal revolutionary wholly satisfied with the mere knowledge that they are doing the right thing. The very poor may need to be given basic subsidies, but as soon as is feasible these should be replaced by suitably and palpably rewarded jobs. Mujica's anarchist preferences do not make him anti-work, but under capitalism anyone who is required to devote part of their time to toil must be paid adequately enough to avoid the sensation of being exploited or sacrificed to it while working hard enough in exchange to deserve the compensation received.

With only limited capacity to generate the necessary resources, this will not be easy, however: 'the idea of solidarity and income redistribution cannot result in economic paralysis.' Consequently, Mujica will court entrepreneurs of big and small business, but sees the state as obliged to lead by example: 'I know that Uruguay needs a revolution, a revolution in management, in commitment. I don't know whether we have the guts and the will for it. It's not a question of the State being too big or too small. It suffers from paralysis, it's got to be made to work usefully . . . Fire fighters need to stop treading on their own hoses. It's a hard fight, a struggle for participation and convenience of and for all, a fight for stimuli and encouragement that are seen as accessible. Participation has to come down to earth from its asexual limbo of abstraction.' It is hard to decide whether the 'we' here is the Uruguayan people as a whole or a left government, but it is clear that a reformed state must lead the fight for the creation of an accepted culture of purposeful work well done and well paid. Reforming the inefficiencies of a cumbersome state apparatus is a constant theme in Uruguayan politics, and not only on the left, but getting such change implemented has proved an uphill struggle for all so far. 'The problem [Mujica believes] is to avoid the sclerosis of bureaucratism because the triumph of bureaucracy is the triumph of sclerosis . . . We have to look for new ways forward because the State needs reforming from top to bottom, because bureaucracy is worse than the bourgeoisie, is a kind of degenerate bourgeoisie that contributes nothing, has no creative energy but just lies and pretends. Bureaucracy is the most exquisite form of exploitation. And we can't hide away from this problem because through not having a really socialist program, the left is more exposed to it: becoming a more or less modernised bureaucracy with better technology is just another way of becoming absorbed into it.' Mujica's praise of the bourgeoisie's energy and creativeness in contrast to the dead weight of a bureaucracy that slows everything to a near halt is, of course, much quoted and recalls his opinion cited earlier that the Soviet bloc collapsed in part because the state apparatus had become an enemy of the people in whose name it was supposed to be functioning. It is unsurprising then to find him in 2009 defending capitalism's success in recognising the 'one in ten or fifteen people' who are natural leaders: 'We fall into too rationalist a concept of democracy when we say we are all going to be equal; no, we are not equal. We are similar; so in public administration or any other enterprise, we have to look for these guys and try to influence them to influence others.'

Mujica understood how influential bureaucracy was in the mindset of all Uruguayans, including his own, because of the legacy of the paternalist Batllista state and its aim of ensuring the welfare of the country's citizens from birth to funeral: 'We are formed in strictly hierarchic societies and we don't see there are other forms of hierarchy, horizontal hierarchy, the accumulation of all collective input.' This must always be kept in mind: 'Bureaucracy tends to concentrate power, but that's silly . . . We have to protect ourselves against a historical inertia that develops and eventually becomes what really governs us.' Mujica contrasted the 1980s social movements with the party organisation he grew up with: 'The young rejected formal organizational stability.' They had a 'horizontality' that 'functioned through assemblies, changing every day, as a cushion against whatever differences might turn up among them. Nothing to do with the way we used to function . . . we were formal and tragic while they have a behaviour that is apparently anarchic but has a profound internal logic.' Clearly expressed here is Mujica's admiration for the informal communal gathering that changes shape and function according to the needs of the moment, having no formal structure or leadership that can lead to internal power struggles over who is to occupy a position such as General Secretary and the like. But he also recognises that while this may be fine for student uprisings (as in 1968) or general citizen insurrections, it is not going to work for a left government in modern Uruguay: 'We need to widen participation in decision making at the local level but that raises the problem of who actually takes the decisions and assumes responsibility for them', but a start can be made at the local level: 'If you've got a job to do in a particular neighbourhood, use workers and businesses from the same neighbourhood because they know the area and the people and will have to front them if they get things wrong.' Indeed, ever since the first Broad Front administration in the city of Montevideo there have been neighbourhood meetings to draw up priorities when allotting budget allowances to local projects.

'We need a bureaucracy that has a tangible moral responsibility for things, that puts the meat on the barbecue and is seen to be doing it.' What Mujica in effect recommends and desires is a public service with a sense of duty towards the citizens it serves and whose taxes pay the public servants' salaries because 'decentralisation of decision making' implies 'the assumption of responsibilities': 'Reliable staff are going to have a confrontation with society over ethics because we can't flatter people, tolerate things or go over towards punishment, but rather along the route to attraction and motivation. We need to promote a desire to emulate, to make our enthusiasm infectious.' There would be serious brakes on this vision splendid because among workers and in their trade unions 'there is often a corporatist vision rather than one based on class.' In other words, workers and those employed in their organisations' bureaucracies protect themselves first. They might object to cutting overtime to employ more people, while politicians – including those from his own Broad Front party – would reject Mujica's attempts to get them to set an example by cutting salaries and some privileges such as the unrestricted use of ministerial cars. And even decentralisation had its limits: the Town Hall in Montevideo 'made a poetic mistake . . . Who said that in this society of ours people want to participate?' Studies of the Montevideo council's experiments with decentralisation suggest the level of participation is not always what might be hoped. Some citizens are no doubt just too busy or too tired to attend, while others either trust their representatives to do budget allocations or at the very least think they should do what they are paid to do. As Mujica accepted in 2009, the average workers do not want extra responsibilities; they 'just want to do their hours and go home.' Anyone can try to set an example; but they can't oblige anyone else to follow it.

These caveats raise the whole issue of political representation, a matter that, as we have already seen, is never far from Mujica's thinking on political matters, especially since 1994 when he became for the first time precisely that, an elected representative in parliament, a position very much at odds with what we have seen him call 'the values of the old anarchists.'

Parliament and the Problem of Representation

Mujica is in two minds about parliamentary democracy. On the one hand he has the anarchist revolutionary's inevitable doubts about what or whom, if anything, the elected representative can actually represent. On the other, he can see, especially after gaining some experience there of his own in both houses on the opposition benches and then more on the government side, that aspects of the parliamentary system of government are useful in certain specific areas, given the ways in which capitalist society tends to work. Consequently, he has 'no time for these pseudo-revolutionaries who get into parliament and then in the name of revolution criticise it for being reformist when that's what it does', and he correctly points out that 'so-called parties with revolutionary intentions have often fought at the level of reforms when they have an institutional character and presence in Parliament. They then stop questioning the system in the interests of making improvements . . . Some have defined revolution as a collection of reforms . . . Revolutionaries can opt for a reformist stance for tactical purposes, to avoid being wiped out, or to link up with the masses.' As Mujica here makes clear, such a view implies renouncing any revolutionary desire to overthrow the system and replacing it with the more moderate hope of reforming it from within. After all, the French Revolution of 1789, the most famous of all revolutions in Western Europe, abolished the feudal state and the absolutist monarchy but not the parliament, which, extended and transformed by a new and more liberal-democratic constitution, became the foundation of the first French bourgeois republic. Of course, a hostile commentator might point out that this did not prevent the rise of Napoleon and his dynasty.

Nevertheless, having said that, Mujica's doubts about the viability and principle of political representation still appear to dominate his thinking about the preferable ways of organising social life: 'Is the idea of representation, of delegation, in crisis? . . . I ask myself whether this institutional paragraph they have constructed, representative democracy, won't have to change over time. . . . Representation may be inevitable, but must it be of the kind we have had up to now?' And again: 'People swallow the representation line too easily; one can end up actually thinking you represent someone. For me this is absurd, whatever the Constitution may say, and in this I believe I am still a libertarian. Nobody represents anybody', while he is particularly severe on the existence of the Senate or any kind of Upper House: 'I think having a Senate is paying a tribute to nobility. I even see it as almost anti-Republican, lower and upper house, it creates a hierarchy . . . And it doesn't improve the quality of parliament's work.' The reference to Mujica himself as a libertarian can serve as a reminder that, although the Revolution of 1789 did not question but confirm the legitimacy of parliamentary representation, it was the Paris Commune of Spring 1871 that experimented with forms of working class anti-parliamentarian self-government which Kristin Ross groups together despite their differences under the heading 'Anarchist Communism.' Moreover, Alain Badiou in his *Of an Obscure Disaster* can be said to fill out Mujica's critique of representative democracy in his 1991 account of its apparent triumph over the whole Communist idea after the fall of the neo-Stalinist bloc in 1989–1991: 'Let us agree to call our democracy... capital-parliamentarianism. The underlying hypothesis on the discourse on the triumph of democracy would then be the following: . . . Capital-parliamentarianism is the unique mode of the political, the only one to combine economic efficiency (and thereby the profit of owners) with popular consensus. If one takes this hypothesis seriously, one must agree that henceforth... *capital-parliamentarianism serves, by political definition, the whole of humanity* [Badiou's italics] . . . is the ultimate political form finally found in which the whole of humanity is reasonably fulfilled . . . that capital-parliamentarianism is commensurable with the very Idea of humanity. This is precisely what the philosopher cannot grant.' Nor could Mujica, though he can see that parliament has its uses.

Speaking some ten years after Badiou was writing on the shock to the left of the events of 1989 and some seven years after beginning his stint as opposition deputy, Mujica could accept some of the parliamentary system's positive features that Badiou's necessarily fierce polemic response to the West's 1990s triumphalism could not afford to allow. For Mujica the personal touch is all-important: 'Parliament votes laws but their content is decided more in face-to-face meetings. A meeting between [the President and opposition party leaders] is worth more than the General Assembly.' Similarly, 'the real work of parliament is done in the committees, which is where people are asked to appear. You see the whole selection there, amazing individuals, and you see that society has a reserve of people and knowledge that is enormous, a panoply so wide as to be difficult to measure anywhere else. This formative aspect of Parliament is the one most worth preserving.' Meeting and understanding whole swathes of Uruguayans he would be unlikely to come across in any other walk of life is crucial in Mujica's experience of the usefulness of parliament: 'I travel a lot more all round the country, and I feel much more a part of it now. That has opened things up for me, because the country is not institutionalised in the Constitution; it's institutionalised in people's heads.' This notion is an almost perfect translation of Benedict Anderson's idea of the nation as 'Imagined Community', a more or less consensual or collective ideological construct that is open to challenge and change, albeit only slowly and accumulatively, especially in and through the media. As Mujica has said, 'parliament has a useful role as a place to denounce corruption and injustice, but a genuinely free press would do it much better . . . Exposure helps form public opinion, and public opinion is the real brake on things.'

This concept of a generally held but not necessarily wholly conscious idea of a national culture that is almost myth brings Mujica back to the theme of participation in its construction in an attempt in 2002 to sum up his view of the role of what goes on in Uruguay's Palacio Legislativo: 'Parliamentary government shows what Parliament's real role is because the Executive is in some way subject to it . . . Parliament shouldn't be hung up in the cloakroom. I don't want to do an apology for dictatorship or any other concentration of power. Quite the opposite . . . I think societies should decentralise much more, and I would like to think that the inevitable massification if not of culture then of knowledge, made possible through the revolution in computers and information technology, will bring conditions for the functioning of society that are unimaginable now, forms of direct participation that can't even be thought of now.'

By 2009, after having served as a minister and in the middle of his electoral campaign for the presidency, Mujica had suspended his thinking on the more general aspects and was focusing on just one aspect: 'Politics in a representative system is permanent negotiation . . . negotiation with social forces, between and within political parties, with the country's business corporations, which all bring different ways of seeing reality. You have to go with the result you get out of it all and not think that you know the way and it's the only route you're prepared to take.' Mujica accepted that he was no longer looking to build socialism by doing this, despite 'the other left that beats up on us and says we have become traitors.' He was one of those who thought that 'capitalism has to function the best way possible' by which he meant whatever was necessary 'to aid in the conceptual, cultural and scientific enrichment of society as a whole.' 'We are putting our bets on change within the game of liberal democracy. That's what we're up to, because if we aren't, we're just a contradiction on legs.' In this 'game', even the Senate was useful: 'it's the natural setting for political contact between parties', since as president he would have to be able to talk to any and everyone. Consequently, he wanted his opponents to be able to say that 'if the Broad Front is going to win, we hope we get Pepe because at least we know we can talk to him', thereby 'keeping in touch with the government'.

They would get him, and a slogan on a Montevideo wall could proudly proclaim: 'A Pepe in every century'. Referring to the three centuries since independence from Spain, the slogan painter pointed to José 'Pepe' Artigas, Uruguay's national hero celebrated as founder of the nation at the beginning of the nineteenth century, José 'Pepe' Batlle y Ordóñez, the creator of the Uruguayan welfare state at the begiining of the twentieth, and José 'Pepe' Mujica at the start of the twenty-first. Mujica might prefer to be forgotten but it seems unlikely that others will agree with him. Still, it is too early to know what Mujica will be best remembered for, but some hints will be forthcoming in this book's next and final chapter, which will focus on his stints as minister and president, how he got there and the thinking that accompanied him along the way.

CHAPTER THREE

MUJICA AS PRESIDENT

M[ujica]: *You will see the Left in government.*
I[nterviewer]: *I'm not very optimistic.*
M: *Yes, you will.*
I: *I mean I'm not very optimistic about what I'll see.*
M: *Ah, yeah, well. That makes two of us.*

[2002]

What the creation of ideas most needs is freedom and respect, because it's an exchange. However, being in government is not very conducive to such things.

José 'Pepe' Mujica [2003]

The organic link between the private ownership of the means of production, or rather, radical structural inequality, and "democracy" is no longer a theme for socialist polemics but the rule of consensus. Yes, Marxism wins: the underlying determining foundations of parliamentarism, its necessary *link with capitalism and profit, are exactly what Marxism always said they were .*

Alain Badiou [1991]

I see the Left of the future as an educational tool toiling away in society's corners. But if it doesn't work, we may get its opposite, as people begin to think the way they live when it should be the reverse: we should live the way we think.

José 'Pepe' Mujica [February 2015]

When Raúl Sendic, the iconic founder and intellectual progenitor of the original Tupamaros guerrilla Movement of National Liberation [MLN], emerged physically and emotionally damaged from the military's jail in March 1985 he brought with him a very basic axiom that would underpin the post-dictatorship MLN's participation in mainstream Uruguayan politics: they would play the liberal democratic election game 'with no cards up their sleeve.' In other words, there would be no threat of hidden guns despite their possible vulnerability to vengeful elements of the military. As Sendic himself would put it in 1986 in one of the very few public speeches he ever made (his wounds and the perhaps deliberately indifferent medical treatment he received in captivity had left him with a serious speech impediment): 'There is a certain mentality in this country. We do not live in a country that has a Tsarist past, as was the case in the Soviet Union, nor one presided over by Mandarins as China had been. We have a strongly rooted democratic tradition in the mentality of the people, a tradition of liberties, and we need to adapt socialism to Uruguay's reality. [We need] a form of socialism that is compatible with that tradition, which we might call libertarian, innate in the Uruguayan people.' As Mujica has repeatedly reminded us when questioned, Sendic was against the idea of the conventional political party, always preferring the concept of the much less organised 'movement'. He was the leading light behind the first publication in Uruguay of the works of the renegade early twentieth-century German socialist Rosa Luxembourg; he disagreed with the Lenin's and the Bolsheviks' reading of Marx and went to Cuba only to quarrel openly with the revolutionary government there on the question of Soviet influence. Sendic's freedom to express his disagreement even with his mentors and teachers was what led Mujica to define him as a 'heretic', a word that could describe not only Mujica's own approach to political matters before he was imprisoned but also his way of being a formally elected member of parliament after 1994.

It was on this understanding of the need to look for new, freer ways of conducting political activity that, beginning the day after their release, Mujica and other MLN heavyweights who had been the military's 'hostages' for so long began to look for a retreat or sanctuary where they could regroup and plan a strategy for how to proceed. Concurrently, they all began to reinsert themselves back into a normal community life (Mujica started growing and selling flowers again, while his partner Lucía worked in the cafeteria of the Faculty of Architecture where she had begun her own career as an MLN militant years before). The MLN found sanctuary doors open to them, as unlikely as it sounds, in a monastery, and it was from there that they went to their first public meeting where Mujica gave his improvised speech in March 1985 which contained the kernel of the group's discussion of the ideas brought from their earlier exchanges while still confined. This speech was used to introduce Mujica's approach to politics and philosophy in Chapter Two.

This final chapter rounds off the story by tracing first the outline of Mujica's career as militant and politician in the Uruguay that had recovered its democratic traditions and needed to rebuild and consolidate its civil society, offering along the way a brief account of how the Tupamaros guerrilla leaders and their supporters (but not all of either) turned themselves into the most voted sector within the centre left Broad Front ruling party, as well as a preliminary assessment of the successes and failures of his periods first as a minister and then as the nation's president. We shall then see how Mujica's increasing commitment to legality and his experience of the exercise of real power within it modified and refined his ideas on how a reconstructed left might be able to offer real alternatives in a globalised (and still-globalising) world in which some combination of parliamentarianism and international capitalism was and remains the only realistic game in town. It would be the way he put together his own way of living, his growing stature as government member and leader and his thinking on how we all might fix a world that seemed only to lurch from crisis to crisis that fuelled his ever-growing public persona, first at home and then abroad. As Mujica put it in April 2009 at the end of a presidential campaign speech, improvised as usual, to an invited audience of intellectuals, writers, teachers and sundry other cultural workers: 'Good faith is the only thing I'm intransigent about. Almost all the rest is negotiable. Thanks for accompanying me.' In a nutshell: commitment, negotiation, solidarity. But the really essential word here will turn out to be that apparently inoffensive 'almost'.

Uruguay after the Deluge

The MLN's activities following its leaders' release took place against the background of Uruguay's transition from dictatorship to democracy under the first of four conservative, middle-of-the-road governments by the traditional parties: three Colorado party administrations (1985–1990, 1995–2000, 2000–2005), the first two under the same president (Julio María Sanguinetti) but separated by a single National Party administration (1990–1995) under president Luis Lacalle, who would be Mujica's main rival in 2009, while the third Colorado president was Jorge Batlle. It would be Batlle who on 1 March 2005 handed the presidential sash on to Tabaré Vázquez, the first time any party other than the Colorados or the

Nationals was elected to govern Uruguay in its entire history as an independent nation, and the first of the Broad Front centre-left governments that still run the country with Vázquez again at the helm until 2020. Readers are reminded that presidential and legislative elections take place in the October/November prior to the formal ceremony of handing over power that is always on the first day of March the following year.

What follows in the next few paragraphs is not intended as even a potted history of the twenty-five years separating Mujica's freedom in March 1985 under the amnesty for all political prisoners approved unanimously in parliament under the first Sanguinetti government and his own assumption as national president in 2010 following the first of Vázquez's presidencies. However, it does seek to fill in some necessary background to an assessment of Mujica's actual performance as minister and president as opposed to merely evaluating his ideas and hopes regarding politics and the exercise of power by the left in a capitalist world. And, indeed, the first and most important question of all is economics, for when the Broad Front took over the reins of government in 2005 it had to continue what was at that point a slow recovery from the country's worst economic collapse since the worldwide depression of the 1930s. In 2001–2 the River Plate region, after a slowdown that had begun two or three years earlier, experienced a foretaste of what would happen to the developed world as a whole in 2007–8. A combination in Argentina of governmental ineptitude (some would add corruption) and unrestrained laissez-faire market economics brought the country to its financial knees with even much of its middle classes reduced almost overnight to beggary. As every Uruguayan is bought up to repeat, if Argentina catches a cold, Uruguayans get the flu, and in 2002 a vulnerably over-dollarised Uruguay replicated their big neighbour's situation, suffering a 250% devaluation of its peso, ensuring that the vast majority of Uruguayans who received incomes in pesos, whether workers or their employers, could no longer pay mortgages and debts contracted when the dollar was cheap. Businesses collapsed, unemployment rocketed, properties and homes were lost and many people had to rely on charity for food. The boom that predictably followed this bust would benefit the Broad Front governments, at least until growth began to slow around 2011 as the long-term global effects of the United States' sub-prime crisis of 2008 and the deceleration of the Chinese economic boom tightened the market for Uruguay's primary product exports. All the left's – including Mujica's – doubts about the benefits of unregulated capitalism for ordinary people seemed confirmed. Moreover, as the economy section in a recent survey of Uruguay between 1960 and 2010 coordinated by Benjamín Nahum concluded, even the boom years following the 2002 crash could not bring to a halt the draining through emigration of not just a few of the nation's most valuable people in terms of age, potential and qualifications. This persistent emigration keeps a population at stubbornly stable levels approximating to only just over an economically insufficient three million, thereby raising once again serious questions about the viability of Uruguay as an independent nation that in the last half of the nineteenth century and well into the twentieth had annually received thousands of immigrants from the poorer countries of Europe. The whole issue reiterates a theme encapsulated in the title of the famous 1967 book, Alberto Methol Ferré's *Uruguay as a Problem* [*El Uruguay como problema*] that, as already mentioned in Chapter 1, was republished in 2015. It advocated an accord between Brazil and Argentina as the forerunner to a Latin American federation of nations as the only viable way of securing the continent's viability and stability (and those of Uruguay within it, of course) against the distortions threatened by the influence of foreign powers, rather as the powerhouses of France and Germany could be the only possible root of any strong European union to rival the interests of the United States or China. Such considerations colour the Uruguayan left and Mujica's view of the region – and their hopes for and disappointments with the organisations (such as MERCOSUR and UNASUR, that look to regional integration and cooperation, on the economic and political levels, respectively) that are supposed to promote its unity. If available publications are any guide, all this is less a concern for the right since they are content to rely more on the machinations of international capitalist economics and trade agreements with major and minor world powers to solve – or at least decide – such matters one way or another.

We must also mention here some particular matters that would be of special concern to Mujica both in his thinking as well as his government's policies. The first is education, very badly neglected during the dictatorship, especially at the secondary and tertiary levels, because of staff and students' active role in what the military saw as insurrectionist militancy supportive of the MLN guerrilla or the left in the years prior to the 1973 coup. While staff sacked for political reasons by the military were reinstated after 1985, funding for public education remained low and efforts to modernise, decentralise and de-bureaucratise the entire school education system, whether from the centre-right or centre-left, remain largely stymied to this day. This is so partly because the measures needed, no matter how conceived, exceed the funding available, and partly because the corporatist union representatives of underpaid and under-trained staff understandably but frustratingly defend them against the possible consequences for them of any really meaningful attempts to create an efficient public education system adequate to the times Uruguayans live in.

The second big issue is poverty. Income redistribution was not high on the list of priorities for any of the more conservative administrations after 1985, and the Broad Front governments of Vázquez and Mujica sought to redress the situation, especially after the effects of the 2002 crisis. As Mujica understood, however, handouts cannot be a permanent answer, as important as they are in solving the immediate problems of the indigent. More long-term solutions through tax reform, self-help programs and tripartite agreements on salaries and prices between employers, employee and government representatives have had only limited success. Moreover, since education is seen as one of the ways the young might find a way out of poverty, Mujica's honesty and personal sense of shame at not being able to do more on these two related vital issues will be seen in the pages that follow to be consistent with the emphasis and philosophical approach he brings to them.

A third issue of great importance to the Broad Front in general — and within it the Socialists, Communists and Tupamaros fellow travellers in particular — has been that of bringing the demands of truth and justice to bear on those responsible for what are termed crimes against humanity (such as extra-judicial assassination and the use of torture methods in interrogations) against political prisoners during the dictatorship and in the years immediately leading up to it. In Uruguay, unlike Argentina, the number of permanently disappeared and presumed dead left-wing activists was always relatively small, there remaining today relatively few still open cases. On the other hand, since the combined military and police security forces, especially after the mid to late 1960s, did not distinguish between clandestine guerrilla warriors like Mujica and student or trade union militants engaged in activities considered legal under the Uruguayan Constitution (among whom members of the groups singled out above were a majority), the inhumane treatment of often illegally detained political prisoners remains a hot issue even today. The whole matter is complicated in the Uruguayan case because in 1986 the first Sanguinetti Colorado government, after what was in effect a negotiated transition from military to civilian rule, granted the military what amounted to a guarantee of impunity for any such crimes committed in course of their 'duty.' What is more, when the Uruguayan electorate had the chance to overturn this law by plebiscite in 1989 and again in 2009, they rejected the opportunity in both instances, though only by a small number in the second case. This has meant that it has been fairly easy for attempts to overturn the impunity law by decree or act of parliament to be declared unconstitutional and against the people's wishes, leaving those pursuing the cause of justice in this matter no option but to proceed in the courts on a case-by-case basis. This strategy has had some successes, with several retired generals and colonels, as well as the first civilian president who collaborated with the military at the time of the coup in June 1973, either in prison or under house arrest.

As time passes, the impracticalities of bringing perpetrators to justice mean that this aspect is inevitably and perhaps justifiably replaced by the need to make the truth available to the public. Investigations on this front have discovered unrecorded and informal graves in the grounds of army barracks leading to the identification of some of the 'disappeared', while non-government organisations often started by relatives have turned up children who were born in captivity and adopted out to hide their origins. (The 1986 Argentine feature film *The Official Story* remains a splendid fictional treatment of the personal and political dramas involved in such cases.) The much publicised case of Argentine poet Juan Gelman (like Mujica, also a guerrilla fighter) and his search for his granddaughter Macarena, who was eventually traced alive and well in Uruguay, kept such very human stories in the public eye and mind. A people's right to the truth about important and controversial periods of their nation's history seems morally and intellectually unassailable, while, as the Germans discovered with regard to the Holocaust during their 1950s recovery from defeat in the Second World War, rebuilding a nation on foundations made of lies and silence was, in the end, unsustainable. Mujica's frequently repeated benign, pragmatic and somewhat off-hand approach to all these matters is as unpopular as it is unusual: he was a guerrilla warrior engaged in a fight to control the state and knew what the consequences would be for himself and his comrades if they were defeated, which they were. He and they paid a high price for their loss but, while this history should not be forgotten, concern with it should not be allowed to dominate either the present or the future. Unsurprisingly, such views are not enough for the families of those whose whereabouts and fate are still unknown. The pressures to release all still available files and archives for public perusal so the truth can be known look set to continue unabated for as long as they remain unsatisfied.

From Deputy and Senator to Minister

It is against this general background that the fortunes and vicissitudes of the legalised MLN and of the role of Mujica's brand of militancy within it as part of a reformed and revamped Broad Front must be analysed and assessed. Sendic had brought with him from prison the idea for a political front that would be to the left of the existing Broad Front but would include it in a an even wider framework, the embodiment of a transformed and legalised MLN devised in prison by himself and other leading members of the organisation. At the same time the leaders of the MLN began to travel the country, holding informal gatherings wherever they went at which they would drink 'mate', the local River Plate bitter tea, and hold conversations with anyone who turned up. They had realized how cut off from the current reality of what Uruguay was their long captivity had left them, and decided that listening to and asking questions of the ordinary folk they met on their travels throughout the country was probably the best way to start catching up on both the state of things and the mood of the populace. Mujica saw this formative period as essential to his subsequent development as militant, spokesman and politician, in part because he discovered that the MLN's reputation had penetrated more deeply into many sectors of the population than they realized and, what is more, had only been enhanced by their enforced absence from society. The military's strategy had backfired: incarceration and martyrdom had not consigned the Tupamaros and their leaders to oblivion but rather raised them to almost mythic status, suggesting, even ensuring, they would have at least the beginnings of a potential electorate once they were in a position to reach out to it. Indeed, they could raise a little money selling reprints of internal documents from their 1960s guerrilla days because so many people wanted to have a signed copy!

While Sendic's notion of some kind of front even more inclusive than the existing Broad Front would, perhaps predictably, not prosper (being seen as an attempt to either confuse people or to kidnap or supplant the already at least partially successful one), it indicated a change of style and tone. The MLN was now open to alliances with others who might not be socialists but had a national liberation approach to what was going to become the dominant trend in government from the late 1980s onwards in Uruguay, Latin America and much of the Western World: a neoliberal market-determined economics that sought to privatize state services, reduce taxes for corporations and the rich, minimize all state intervention and formal welfare for the poor, unemployed and the sick. This flexibility of alliances against a common foe was both a tool for mobilizing people and one of the premises behind an MLN committed to electoral democracy that requested formal entry into the Broad Front coalition in April 1986. This was not granted until three years later, the long wait an indication both of changes inside the Front in part brought on by the controversy caused within it by MLN's request, but also of the long-standing mutual distrust between the two movements going back to the half-hearted support offered to the fledgling Front by the MLN in the 1971 elections.

Early 1989 saw the creation of the Movement for the People's Participation [MPP], a more radically left voting bloc within the Broad Front that followed Sendic's original idea of all-inclusiveness in being based around the MLN but bringing in smaller groups, a few 'independents' and renegades from the Colorado or National parties. Both Mujica and his then partner Lucía Topolansky – they would marry only in 2005 – were leading members from the start of an MPP that would prove essential in the decade to come in ensuring that the Front could retain its left-wing credentials while moderating its program and its rhetoric. In addition to Sendic (who died in April 1989), the figure that would come to symbolise this current within the MLN would be José 'Pepe' Mujica, who could in many ways epitomise the internal changes undergone by the MLN in its transformation into the MPP: he had been a guerrilla fighter in the 1960s and later a member of the MLN executive, a political prisoner for the whole of the dictatorship, and was in the process of becoming, unpredictably from such a starting point, an elected deputy from 1994 and senator from 1999, a minister from 2005, and the country's president from 2010 to 2015! His attractive, deliberately rustic style would make him the most recognised and most electorally popular figure on the Broad Front's left, as well as one of its most interviewed and humorously articulate spokesmen.

Mujica's abilities in this sphere of communication were not only immediately useful in a media-driven world of electoral politics where a candidate becomes a sellable commodity, however. The MPP had a difficulty never faced by the original MLN: how to implement its proposals. The MLN was going to take power by force of arms, but by definition the MPP could not do this, leaving open the question of what would replace revolutionary violence as its methodology. The name of the group suggests the answer: the only method more powerful than a bullet is consensus, and the only way to agreement by all is constant negotiation between as many as possible of all involved parties. The aim of the MPP was and remains, then, to be a vehicle for popular participation in the sense of being constantly flexible enough (a 'movement') to incorporate an ever wider proportion of the left (and beyond) who could be convinced through persuasion to the point that their principle of social inclusiveness and the elimination of socio-economic difference in the name of equal opportunities for all would survive the vicissitudes and arbitrariness of voting patterns every few years. In this context, Mujica's thoughts on modern China just over half way through his presidency in September 2013 acquire a relevance much closer to home. In effect, Mujica thought, the peculiar combination in China of a Communist Party leading a regulated market economy depended on two concepts: an imposed meritocracy added to a tendency many centuries in the making, a 'swarm mentality' [in Mujica's Spanish, 'cultura colmenar'] that had always led the Chinese to think it better to follow rather than oppose government planning, an attitude going back to the earliest imperial period. Mujica goes on revealingly: '[China], you might say, is the only place where government gives the orders but they don't control everything because they're authoritarian; they can give orders because they know they will be obeyed, which is different.' Indeed it is, and since nothing must upset the functioning and improvement of the 'swarm' and its activities, it also indicates why the Chinese Communists are so hard on those seen as enemies (and why the liberal democratic West supports such 'dissidents'). In the end, Mujica's and the MPP 's idea of popular participation as increased social inclusiveness would, in some future world, in effect bypass the rotation of parties in power so dear to the practice of liberal democracy. As expressed in an MPP document from 1996, cited by Mazzeo as one of most important points of reference for the MPP's political strategy, 'to accept being a minority is, among other things, to accept that the road to national liberation is long and pluralist, and will become a reality WHEN WE WIN OVER A MAJORITY [capitalised in the document] not because everyone becomes part of our organisation but because revolutionary ideas will have won over the consciousness of a majority.' The 'swarm', that image much used by Mujica and borrowed from the natural world for which he feels such affection and affinity, would be self-sustaining in the sense that no opposition group could win a majority in even the freest and most transparent elections because there would be insufficient interests left unaddressed by the 'swarm' to ever allow a majority to prevail over it. The MPP, in the long run, seeks the old MLN-Tupamaros socialist revolution by other means! To abuse Alain Badiou a little, everyone would be a philosopher who could see that all his or her highest hopes for individual development and happiness could best be brought about by working as part of the 'swarm' rather than against it.

Of course, not everyone saw this or thought this way in the 1980s, and the MLN's application to join the Broad Front in April 1986 created divisions not only within the Broad Front, where it caused realignments and some at least temporary defections. The legalised MLN itself was riven by debates about its aims and ideology, and the most implacable opponent of the new move to become more accommodating in its approach to Uruguayan liberal democracy was termed a 'proletarian' trend, one increasingly at odds with both the new MLN and the Broad Front, especially as the latter as a whole became more openly a post-socialist centre-left reformist party. The 'proletarians' had a more traditionally Marxist-Leninist conception of the people and of working class and trade union politics, and even secretly evolved plans for a 'politico-military organisation' to lead an armed population in resisting any attempt at a military coup like that of June 1973. The theoretical underpinnings of the 'proletarians' extended from quasi-Leninist to libertarian, but at its inception it included some MLN founders or elders, although never Mujica himself. In 1987, he could be found anticipating the shape of things to come: 'No change is possible without cultivating a humble policy in which each one of us occupies his or her place or without the wisdom needed to advance slowly as a vast multi-party, democratic group that respects popular participation. Our still undecided request for admission to the Broad Front is a strategic move in this regard.' At roughly the same time as Mujica was advocating this watered down version of Sendic's all-inclusive front, the MLN's 'proletarians' were reaching their apogee. Around 1989 they controlled all the major MLN and MPP media outlets (publications and radio station), only being gradually displaced during the 1990s as the ever-improving electoral fortunes of the Broad Front (and the growing popularity of the MPP and Mujica within it) gradually convinced the leaders and members of both MLN and MPP that they could share power in an elected centre-left government under the umbrella of the Encuentro Progresista [Progressive Meeting]. This moderately reformist catchall movement, which Mujica saw as modelled on Sendic's ideas, was created in 1994 by Tabaré Vázquez, who would successfully use it to propel himself and the Broad Front into government (and Mujica into a ministry) in 2005. Mujica might be able to say with equanimity that 'we used to want to change the world but now we just want to fix the pavement in front of our house', but many MLN members, discomforted by the all but total abandonment of the movement's original program and methodology, left the new parliament-oriented MPP in disagreement if not, as in some cases, disgust.

Indeed, it has been argued that it was the violent actions in August 1994 by the MLN 'Proletarians' in support of Basque Nationalist militants who were to be extradited to Spain to stand trial for supposed terrorist activities that lost Vázquez the presidency in that year's national elections. The Colorado Party won in a poll that all but portrayed the country as a constituency divided into three equal parts for the first and only time in the nation's history. The two traditional parties learnt their lesson: they joined forces to vote through a constitutional change in 1996 one consequence of which was the introduction of a second round as a straight run-off between the two most voted presidential candidates if no party received more than fifty percent in the first general ballot. This kept Vázquez out of office once more in 1999 when the Colorado party won again in a second round vote, but not on the last Sunday of October 2004, when the Broad Front managed a first round win with a majority in both houses of Montevideo's Legislative Palace. This crowned a trend in which the centre-left had increased its vote in every election since it first arrived on the scene in 1971 (the twelve-year dictatorship only postponing the inevitable, it seems), a gradual upward movement that enabled it to take power in Montevideo's Town Hall in 1989 and retain it till today, as well as to develop its mobilising capacity nationally by organising successful campaigns against the sell-off of publicly owned entities during the 1990s. The always active militant Mujica went on the streets and public transport as a board-wearing sandwich man to publicise the campaign against the conservative government policy.

Mujica finally entered parliament as an opposition deputy on February 15, 1995. A much-repeated anecdote from those early days, later revealed by Mujica himself as apocryphal, suggests just how much at odds with the general tenor of the place and its usual occupants Mujica both felt and was perceived to be. He was reputed to have arrived on a motor scooter that first day and the car park attendant, clearly taking him for a visitor, asked him how long he would be leaving it there, to which Mujica was supposed to have replied: 'Five years, if they let me.' This jarring sense of difference was genuine – the high salaries and ceremonial allure did not blind him to the reasons behind his long held doubts about this system of government in Uruguay – but it also seems true that Mujica quickly learnt how to exploit it as publicity in photographs, interviews and election campaigns. It would appear that he used his time in both houses prior to becoming a minister both in making contacts with old and new deputies and senators from all political camps and with a similar array of political journalists and in doing a lot of work (Mujica's reputation as a tireless worker at what interests him polit-ically and excites him personally is universal) on the two aspects of life as elected representative we have already noted as appearing to him as the most valuable and purposeful. Firstly, he continued the travels round the country to meet the people and see the conditions especially in the rural interior that he had begun in 1985 with the MLN campaign of 'mate' tea conversations and, secondly, Mujica participated actively in parliamentary committees on particular issues where once again he had the chance to meet and listen to a wide cross-section of Uruguayans from all walks of life called to appear as experts or witnesses, while he could also entertain the hope of directly influencing specific policy matters via the committee report process.

On 5 May 1995 Mujica made his maiden speech in the Chamber of Deputies, as Uruguay's lower house is named. He was given thirty minutes on a topic dear to his heart and long-time interests:

'Pasture, Cattle, Humans: Towards a National Policy'. After regaling the House with an exposition on the conditions of rural life ranging from the appalling wages and conditions for the 'forgotten and marginalised' peasants and labourers and their equally bad housing situation to the state acquisition and ownership of productive land, he requested – and received – the House's indulgence for fifteen extra minutes to finish his examination of what he saw as 'a topic that get's little coverage in this place.' He finished with a characteristic flourish: 'I am aware that the matters that arouse this kind of worry are either solved through consensus or not solved at all. We need to do something for this country of ours that is dying in the interior. I have not called my proposals here a State policy, because the State does not belong to everyone. But the Nation does, and that is why this is a national question.' The call for all relevant parties to get together and reach agreement is little short of a mantra for Mujica the negotiator, while the aim (or dream) of closing the gap between the State controlled by a minority and the Nation that is everyone's could be seen as a catch-cry for all Mujica's political endeavours from pretty much the 1950s on.

It was during the four years he spent in the Chamber of Deputies that one day the veteran Socialist deputy Guillermo Chifflet whispered prophetically to Mujica's fellow MLN leader and *de facto* official historian of the Movement, Eleuterio Fernández Huidobro: 'Have you noticed, mate, that when Mujica is speaking here, not even a fly stirs?' It was shortly before becoming a Senator that Mujica came up with of definition of power that shows the clear influence of his first few years in parliament: 'Power is management. Not so much capital, but management. Workers don't know how to manage and they need to learn. Whoever takes on the power to govern must learn the hard craft and commitment involved in managing things.' He then went on to alter radically Lenin's definition of revolution: from 'Soviets plus electricity' Mujica produced a short definition of left-wing government as 'accountancy plus ideologically directed participation.' He then expanded this to mean the idea of taking from capitalism the need to measure both work and its results in order to increase participation as a way of decentralising decision-making: 'give people more power to make decisions themselves . . . Human beings will change precisely to the degree that they are capable of making their own decisions and taking responsibility for them.' To be fair, Mujica would acquire a reputation as minister and president for being creative and astute on policy matters and a fine, patient tactician in negotiations of all kinds but he chafed at the bit on administrative detail and the require-ments of over-bureaucratised implementation and decision-making processes. In other words, he needed a trustworthy team around him to attend to those 'accountancy' matters that in principle were so important to his view of what management should be. Mujica's approach here and elsewhere to this matter is open to dispute, which is how he would like it as for him such concerns are never prede-termined or fixed in stone, but they are concrete examples of what few thinkers on the left have to approach in practice: how to make the transition from being an opposition that criticises both princi-ples and practice of those in power to actually trying to make a real difference by remaining measurably on the left while governing oneself on terrain not of its own making. Mujica's legacy will revolve around this question: to what extent did his administration offer examples or even glimpses of what a left in power might do even though it left largely intact the institutions of liberal democracy and the economic priorities of capitalism?

Once he became Minister for Agriculture under the first Vázquez presidency in the first Broad Front national government in 2005, Mujica could at last do something about those rural questions that had been bothering him ever since his earliest days as a militant based on his experience of the countryside obtained on the Gordano family properties where he went on holidays as a child and teenager and had still occupied first place when he registered for his maiden speech in parliament. What follows is a selection⋆ of his thoughts on the **Rural Interior of Uruguay** and its difficulties taken from interviews before his stint as Minister:

'Really, agrarian reform is a struggle by the bourgeoisie against their feudal masters, but the left has tried to take it towards socialist goals, giving it a more or less collectivist tone.'

On the farming practices at his and Lucía's smallholding: 'Within the limits of our possibilities we are trying here to imitate [the coop-

---

⋆ Mujica's thoughts on the **Rural Interior of Uruguay, Education, Culture, Global Politics, his Socialist Vision** and finally his **World View of History and Globalisation** are provided in set out form in the pages to follow. The quoted material is left in roman type; contextual material is set in italics.

erative methods of the Gordano family at Colonia Estrella in Carmelo]. I'm not sure where it's heading but it's much more motivating than being in the Senate.'

His assessment of rural working life as he had found it: 'A brutal form of exploitation. And not only in Uruguay but the whole world. The agricultural sector everywhere is working for the benefit of the transnational space of knowledge ownership.'

'The worst thing is we don't apply what we know . . . we need to keep the cattle grazing on the paddock as in New Zealand. There too they have a higher average milk production per cow and get more lambs per ewe. We still only get the same amount of calves per 100 cows as we did forty years ago', *whereas* 'in New Zealand the numbers they get in experiments are much closer to the real numbers on the average farm and they get most of their ewes to lamb in spring when there's new grass. Here we do it in the autumn!' *New Zealand, another fertile small country with more animals than people, was a favourite point of comparison for Mujica. Finland was another:* 'Finland changed its economy starting with logging and now exports technology. Uruguay must change on the back of cattle and sheep . . . So which approach is more intelligent, cut up the cow and eat the meat or keep the cow and have it produce more milk? That's the question . . . In the last instance, the worker who generates most surplus value will be the one in a laboratory tunic.'

'I never saw a law work the land. Laws are often full of provisions designed to limit individual discretion. We need more decisions and general behaviour made on the basis of experience.'

'Farming is now so complex in the USA that it's third or fourth on the list of stressful professions.'

'Jorge Batlle around 1996 said that the agriculture problem could be fixed by 100 large enterprises. This was a counter-reform that alienates the land, putting us always in the shadow of the multinationals, for which we end up working as cheap labour. It empties the countryside of country people . . . We produce good fodder and fertiliser. We need to improve it and export it.'

'It's humiliating and irrational that agricultural machinery costing hundreds of thousands of dollars is driven by an operator earning just a few dollars a day.'

In effect, the Mujica view of what the rural interior might do and look like comes down to a relatively small number of requirements based on an assessment of the realities of its history and current situation. Uruguay has the history it does because it developed according to the way cattle inserted into the region combined with the development of capitalism in the country. Extensive cattle farming in conjunction with the world market for its products led to the society of today. For Mujica the basic conflict in the countryside is the problem of land ownership and speculation versus land that produces crops or animals. Huge unused landed estates are the product of the first and an impediment to the second. Land still needs subdividing because it didn't happen enough earlier so he hoped to reinforce the Instituto de Colonización to obtain lands for production and then get decent salaries for those who rent and work them.

Diversification meant lamb meat over wool production, technology to improve rice growing, the restructuring of milk production, boosting citrus production, and discovering how to reconcile trees with animals and produce value-added wood instead of just logs and value-added special animals for particular markets. However, if Uruguay farmers were to compete with the big players, small landholders needed to group together in cooperatives (as in the Gordano family) because they may well not survive if left alone. 'The countryside needs to join together', Mujica has said, to form communal centres and welcome migrants from abroad if they come to build homes and farm the interior. In July 2007, after just over two years as head of the Ministry, he said the following: 'Against general expert opinion in universities, I fervently believe that Uruguay's biggest problem in the future is not its market, its capital or its natural resources but rather the workforce that will take on its agriculture.'

The general verdict on his three and a bit years as Minister of Agriculture (he resigned in 2008 to concentrate on his run for the presidential nomination for the 2009 election) was positive in one direction but negative in another. Mujica's biggest successes, aided by tax relief and a boom in international prices for Uruguayan primary products, were on the side of improving the lot of small farmers and rural workers. The minimum wage was fixed to equal those in cities while salaries in the rural sector as a whole increased around 100% during the five years of the first Broad Front administration (when Mujica was Minister), and deals between farmers and supermarkets brought better returns to the producers, whose debts over the period were very significantly reduced, with about 80% paid off and others favourably renegotiated. This was enough to measurably slow down the migration from countryside to the cities.

The biggest black mark was on ownership of land and enterprises and investment in new projects. Despite his well-publicised thoughts on the subject, Mujica was able to do very little about reducing the amount of foreign investment in either buying land or developing new projects, and many refrigeration and rice processing plants are foreign-owned and frequently the recipients of undeclared state perks. Critics have also said there were few or no legal changes that might stimulate exporters to sell more value-added products. In short, Mujica had concentrated on the short-term goals of improving the quality of life and work conditions for rural producers to keep them on the land, postponing or sacrificing more long-term policy changes. As he expressed it a little later during the 2009 presidential campaign: '[I and the vice-presidential candidate] are agreed on getting 250,000 hectares for the Land Colonisation Institute, more than it's ever had in its whole life . . . this is for the small dairy and cattle farmers in the north. Mind you, it's not a matter of inventing land users but of keeping those already there. The battle is to get people to group together so they can copy what the big guys do; it's either that or go under. In other areas, industrialisation and technological change will do the trick. But in cattle farming, husbandry and dairy, it's not like that. In these areas capital and technology achieve less: a breeding cow is a more personalised, artisanal thing . . . The state rents out the land but retains ownership because, if it doesn't, the land becomes just unproductive real estate and you start the cycle of land accumulation again. We need to modify the legislation to ensure the tenant lives on the land and from what it produces and can't sublet it. The aim is families, because the most valuable thing, apart from what is produced, is the reproduction of a rural labour force. In Uruguay we've been occupied with the breeding of cows; now we've got to begin looking to how we can breed country folk.'

The Presidency and After

Mujica's candidature as President had not been easy to arrange and finalise. First, there were his own misgivings: 'I look terrible, like a greengrocer, I'm old and tired, and I don't have a university degree', he had said in 2008. Julio María Sanguinetti, the conservative Colorado Party former president, would use all parts of this statement in an attempt to discredit Mujica against his always elegantly business-suited 'gentleman' National Party opponent in an article published in the Argentine right-wing broadsheet *La Nación* [*The Nation*], an attack that is perhaps more likely to have rebounded in Mujica's favour than damage his reputation (which in many ways it confirmed!). The same can be said of outgoing president Tabaré Vázquez's recommendation of his middle-of-the-road, steady-as-she-goes Minister of Finance Danilo Astori as his successor, who was already seen in Mujica's MPP and by many Communists and Socialists as putting too many financial brakes on progressive social legislation, although his management of the economy was recognised even by the opposition as having been 'responsible' in the face of the multiple demands of what that same liberal-minded formula regularly and derogatively dismissed – and still dismisses – as 'left-wing populism'. Mujica, too, had complained pungently only a few months after taking on the Ministry of Agriculture that his budget proposals were constantly being rejected 'by Harvard, which is just as dogmatic as Moscow', a shorthand way of saying that Harvard Business School-prescribed recipes were just as hard to alter or resist as those of the Kremlin in Soviet times, hardly a comparison that flattered Astori and his economic team. Nonetheless, after a bruising internal tussle and some very painful negotiating, the Broad Front settled on the only at first unlikely candidature formula of Mujica as President and Astori as his running mate for Vice-President, the former being the creative if slightly whacky bounce to the latter's somewhat stolid sturdiness ('no sex appeal' would be Mujica's pithy summing-up of the public Astori, whereas Mujica himself would end up being able to draw the same kind of audience as Mick Jagger, internationally if not always at home). Meanwhile, Astori could be the often essential prose-of-the-world counterpart to Mujica's usually improvisatory libertarian instincts ('I say what I think and I think what I say'), not always helpful in a national president on the diplomatic or foreign trade fronts.

Mujica and Astori had one big advantage: the people's verdict on the First Broad Front government. Vázquez got an almost unbelievably high (roughly 70%) personal rating on leaving office, while his administration, though much lower, was still well into positive territory. The Mujica–Astori combination could capitalise on the reputation of a government that had begun to make inroads into the decades-old slum poverty on the edges of cities and in the interior, had exploited the economic boom to improve workers' salaries and pensions and to get many into health cooperatives as an alternative to the overburdened free public sector. Vázquez's administration had also given a basic personal computer with free Internet connection to all public schoolchildren (although it remained far from having solved the multiple problems in a long underfunded public education sector, an issue that would be a permanent headache for Mujica's government and remains one today). These issues far outweighed in importance for the average Broad Front voter the less successful record on foreign relations (especially with Argentina and the MERCOSUR countries) or on the sense of insecurity felt on Montevideo's streets (a topic exploited by the media, nearly all friendly to the right) brought about in part by the rise in visible crime, minor and major, which accompanied a policy of social inclusion and the publicised police and prevention measures to contain the destructive social forces such policies inevitably released.

Mujica emotionally expressed the gratitude he saw in the new support during the campaign in poor areas all over Uruguay, from army privates to 'self-employed barefoot peasant labourers': 'I think they got something from the Broad Front government, some are grateful to the Ministry for Social Development – someone had remembered them. I remember the letter Juan Manuel Rosas [nineteenth-century Argentine rural leader or (for the Buenos Aires urban elite) local warlord who became President] wrote to [his wife] Doña Encarnación when he was in the desert, where he tells her this: "Don't forget to help the blacks and the poor when they need it. Help them as much as you can, and you'll discover how strong the loyalty of the humble can be".' Mujica's own thoughts on how social housing could be developed reflect this same sense of aid for the weak, though he is more specific about what he means by 'help': 'You need a creative spirit, you've got to go into the middle of the slums on the city outskirts with an active approach, get the numbers of sole mothers with children etc., and invent a solution for each case. It's not going to be a beautiful house or the square box some want to build . . . It's not just an architecture problem; it's a social question. In some places they build these little square cottages, cut the ribbons at the opening, and then disappear. Nobody thought of the horse the guy's got which, because he's scared it'll get nicked, he keeps in the dining room. No, you need volunteers, activists willing to be in the thick of things, keeping an eye out for the cockups your public servant can make. If there's no militant spirit, don't do it, because it's like throwing money in the sea.' And when asked what remained in 2009 of the Tupamaro who first entered parliament in 1994, he answered: 'There's an eternal question that has to do with equality among human beings, which is ultimately what divides left from right. Over and above this are there are many options but that's the core. The left's way of understanding freedom tends toward equality between human beings, but by equality I mean a frame of reference for the development of the diverse beings we all carry within us. The right has the spirit of competition, the law of the strongest. This contradiction lives on because right and left have complimentary parts in the whole of human history: competition multiplies suffering while the other is more just but risks stagnation. What stays with me of the past is the struggle to make more equal the society in which I live, starting from the base that the main battle is to raise the social sectors at the bottom. How many centimetres will we achieve? I have no idea, but since we live in a capitalist society, the theoretical limit is that the motor of the economy is profit and creativity. How much profit? Enough to keep the economic cycle going, but not as much as capital wants because, otherwise, it won't redistribute wealth. The whole political battle is concentrated on this.' As the recently anointed president put it in his speech to the nation in the open air of Independence Square in the centre of Montevideo on 1 March 2010: 'The subject of change is you, my dear people, with you we will change or with you we will fall.'

In his more official accession speech to the joint houses of Parliament on the same day, Mujica stressed his determination to involve opposition and parliament in the search for ways forward on four long-term problems: security, climate change, energy and education, once again underlining his preference for negotiated agreements, cooperation and collegiate management. He then went on to single out one of the four for special consideration: 'Allow me one emphasis: education, education, education. And once again, education. We who govern should be obliged every morning to fill blank sheets of paper, like in school, writing out a hundred times "I must concern myself with education". That's where we anticipate the face of the society to come. Most of our productive potential as a country depends on education, as does our nation's future capacity to live in daily harmony together.' Given his highlighted preoccupation with this area, it is worth perusing some his thoughts on **Education** before he took on the task of actually building policy aimed at implementing at least some of them:

'In education we are going to have break out of the traditional ways of doing things. Not throw them away but widen them out to be more socially inclusive. I imagine the public school as an assembly where teachers and people are discussing what the program will be, are actually constructing the plan.' *This plan to give individual schools more autonomy on some matters traditionally centralised and controlled by committees with union representation met with all but total resistance by teachers' unions.*

'We've got to appropriate knowledge so it comes to be the superior kind of property . . . we lived through a time of colonization of a territory that was close to us on the left, the area of education . . . Reconstructing the idea of the Nation must be the backbone of our message of political renewal.'

'A country will be more liberated and sovereign the more it owns the knowledge it discovers . . . Possession of knowledge is a form of capital.'

'An education program with all its resources allotted by the State must produce a cultural transformation that brings about different forms of social behaviour, in which in some measure we all become students and teachers for ever.' *As Mujica knew only too well, significant cultural change cannot be accomplished by decree and takes longer than a period of government. I would argue, though, that however little his administration was able to achieve in practice, what it did do under his tutelage was make visible to the whole population that a serious planned alternative to the culture of the status quo was possible, even if it would take several generations and a constantly renewed consensus to bring it about. What Mujica gave Uruguay in this regard was a whiff, a glimpse, of what might be possible if the people could be brought to agree in broad terms on what they wanted.*

'People without a trade or work need to be shown and to learn the benefits of both', *a judgement that covered both high school and post-school vocational training.*

'The teacher finds out about what the people need from working in their midst, and then works with them to build a program that responds to those needs. In that way a teacher is a kind of alarm clock.'

Mujica would expand on this in his speech to the General Assembly of both Houses on the day he took over power: 'In confronting poverty, education is the great source for hope. A school and its teachers are the principle battering ram we must use to integrate those left on the roadside by penury.' *As already mentioned, what Mujica was able to achieve in this area was severely limited, a defeat he would acknowledge and lament with almost tearful honesty.*

Mujica was also capable of this bitter comment on free university education and the undirected state funding of it: 'Autonomy has meant the monstrosity of saying that society must keep out of educational affairs while showing budget solidarity. Solidarity with what? So that we spend fortunes on educating people who then go abroad to work. So we end up subsidising the development of the rich countries that employ them to rip us off.' *Such anger is perhaps explained by the observation that the really big difference between left and right these days revolves around* 'to whom is transferred the ownership of knowledge'. *The limitations of Mujica's success in this area can be accurately measured in a 2013 interview, a couple of years before his presidency's end:* 'My argument to both Germany and the United States is the same: help us educate our people; don't steal them from us. Don't lend us a cent. What we need is brain-power, so don't steal our best brains from us . . . Underdevelopment is first and foremost a mindset issue . . . It's fine that our people go abroad to study. The problem is not having a hook to retain them, so they come back and make their contribution here.'

During the 2009 campaign, he argued that 'we have to bring the

University to the interior, but to do it we need to talk with the people working in education and get them to do it with us, because you can't do it if they are against you'. *As we will see below, Mujica's presidency was unable to secure this cooperation.*

'To have real policies that promote the welfare of the poor, we need the active participation of the reasonably well off, the middle classes. It represents a kind of collegiate leadership in the country. The poor never had the chance to get to the university admission window and if that middle class, the average inhabitant of Pocitos [a relatively well-healed Montevideo beach suburb], does not participate in this sort of cooperative management, we won't be able to be anything except a limited, impoverished country of barbarians.' 'without Pocitos' *but would be unable to govern without the kind of professional that live there. In practice, however, he would have a much harder job convincing the unions and organised labour to cooperate with his streamlining or modernising plans, and education would turn out to be, together with the public service bureaucracy, the area where that resistance was strongest.*

'While the world is demanding more qualifications, we are doing everything in reverse. They talk about Mujica's Slavic model. The Nordic countries spend 7 to 8% of their gross national income on education, and that's from a budget 4 or 5 times bigger than ours. Try competing with that!' *Mujica did secure an improved budget for education but much of it went on getting teachers a decent wage and fixing up deficiencies in school buildings. The planning of a basic school education program that students, teachers, unions and government could agree on awaits both funding and political will.*

A credit and debit entry for the Mujica presidency as a whole might be as follows. Clearly on the credit side would be Mujica's constant determination to be democratic and republican in all his dealings with others, both in and out of the country, and whatever their political hue; the extension of tertiary education institutions into the interior has been welcomed on all sides, if the particular forms it takes are still open to debate; the attempts to build on the first Broad Front government's assault on poverty and slums housing were successful, though did not reach as many families was publicly envisaged. The 'Plan Juntos' ['Together Plan'], a cooperative self-help building project in which future home owners, volunteers and technical and construction specialists combined to build houses in which the future occupiers had a stake that was both personal and economic, did build affordable housing in the capital and elsewhere in the interior, but not in the numbers anticipated. It was criticised by many, including the Broad Front administration that succeeded Mujica's, because its largely informal funding by Mujica himself made its real costs difficult to calculate.

The much publicised progressive legislation on the state cultivation and sale of marihuana (advertised as an experiment in diminishing the ravages of the illegal drug trade), gay marriage, abortion and Afro-Uruguayan representation righted some genuine wrongs and prejudices in Uruguayan society, while the latter's better side was reflected in the help offered to Syrian refugees and to the never tried terrorist suspects incarcerated at Guantánamo, the corner of Cuba never relinquished by the USA and used as a prison not subject to American law (an embarrassment to Barack Obama's Democrat administration and a tug at the heart strings of ex-political prisoner President Mujica). All these measures earned this small nation the 2013 'Country of the Year' vote in *The Economist* ('How bad must the others be?' was the President's own typically terse reaction to the news).

Finally, there was the figure of Mujica himself. As both anti-capitalist theorist on how world society could ensure its survival and an individual who, even as president, lived an authentically anti-capitalist life that did not accumulate money, property or goods, and that was largely self-sustainable through a small farm run cooperatively with neighbours, Mujica became the most eloquent international ambassador there has ever been of an admirable egalitarian Uruguayan republicanism, a status he has still not lost, two years after stepping down from office.

Somewhere in the middle, with entries on both credit and debit sides of the ledger, would be first and foremost foreign relations. Mujica improved but also tested relations with a protectionist, economically strapped Argentina in standing up to its bigger neighbour as they argued over shared water lanes that Uruguay's Finland-owned woodchip industry was supposedly polluting (not so, an international court decided) and over Argentine policies that threatened Uruguay's tourist industry and port services income. Mujica's has always been a loud voice in favour of regional integration and cooperation, but had to face the fact that as the Southern

Cone's common market's two biggest economies, Argentina and Brazil, went into the doldrums, MERCOSUR could not function to Uruguay's advantage, so he sought accords and trade agreements (and investment) elsewhere, in Europe and China especially. He is on record as lamenting Uruguayans' refusal to see themselves as in effect inhabiting a suburb of São Paulo but had to face the fact that some European and Asian countries do not bother with formal diplomatic representation in Uruguay precisely because it is seen as too inevitably tied to Brazilian or Argentine interests.

However, the foreign relations question that best reveals the strengths and weaknesses of Mujica's approach is Venezuela's entry in the MERCOSUR group. There was no valid reason for keeping the oil-rich country out but consensus was required to approve such a matter and the conservative Paraguayan parliament had consistently rejected Hugo Chávez's socialist-leaning, pro-Cuban revolution approach to Latin American affairs, thus preventing Venezuela's entry. When Paraguay was suspended from the group because its right-wing oligarchy illegally overthrew a democratically elected progressive government and imprisoned its president, Mujica teamed up with the other member states to take advantage of Paraguay's absence to get Venezuela in, making at the time one of his most criticised, controversial and most frequently recalled pithy statements: 'Sometimes political considerations must prevail over judicial arguments.' Of course, this was what the Paraguayan government had itself long been doing and what the opportunistic decision against it sought to overturn, but the Uruguayan opposition seek to use it against Mujica's credentials as a democrat, while it is in fact quite consistent with his contention that all law and constitutional documents, rather than neutral permanent stone tablets whose meanings are given and eternally and objectively true, are inevitably ideological reflections of the interests of the individuals or groups who devised them, and therefore are always open to deconstruction, improvement or abandonment. The Uruguayan opposition now invokes the same principles to suspend Paraguay previously called upon to exclude Venezuela, because of the questionable antics of the post-Chávez government's President Maduro. Mujica's view on this is to remain faithful to a friendly nation that sold Uruguay cheap petrol and to hope that all Venezuela's issues can be resolved according to the wishes of its people and the provisions of its constitution, a neutral-sounding formula that in fact reminds Venezuela that it is not post-revolutionary Cuba and that there are limits to what can be imposed to attain socialism under a liberal democratic constitution (which Cuba, of course, no longer has). In other words, if you want to go the revolutionary hog, you have to do it knowingly and openly, but, if unwilling to go that far, you have to accept the limitations of the electoral game, which is what Mujica himself opted to do, a response to a dilemma similar to Maduro's that lost him so much support among the original MLN faithful. Mujica's later views on this are clear and uncomplicated, though whether in principle or self-defence is open to doubt, perhaps: 'Integration is not a matter of left, right or centre; it either is or is not, which is different. This is in conflict with the traditional left. If I want to integrate only with those who resemble me or think like me, there is no integration. No. Integration is with everyone, whatever they're like, or it's not integration at all. This implies a very wide degree of openness.' In other words, for Mujica regional integration is, as in the European Union, between nations, not between governments that come and go.

In the Mujica presidency ledger's wholly debit or negative column would have to be some particular issues: the badly and harmfully bungled wash-up of a failed national airline bled all but dry by private enterprise; unresolved debates between environmentalists, tourism representatives and economists over foreign resourced enterprises such as open cut iron ore mining or a new deep water port, debates whose outlines are familiar to the populations of numerous countries in the world; and the failure to obtain private resources, national or foreign, to invest in an ailing rail system.

Another minus is the situation involving the crimes against humanity during the dictatorship of the 1970s and early 80s. It is arguable that had Mujica, Astori and all the Broad Front parliamentary candidates in the 2009 election openly backed the accompanying referendum to repeal the military impunity law, it would have been passed and the law taken off the statute books. As it is, the referendum was lost by a few percent and the subsequent attempts to change it by law through parliament under Mujica's presidency were predictably rejected as unconstitutional. While this does not mean that individual cases cannot be processed and won for the victims, it has meant that the Supreme Court can see itself as acting on the people's will, while the military can feel tacit support for their defiant resolution to open up neither files nor old wounds. Mujica's subsequent reflections on this matter in September 2013

are substantial and graphic, and worth quoting in full: 'I'm not interested in justice in the historical sense of the term, because it's
impossible; it just doesn't exist. It's the future that interests me and
the fact is the wives and children of the soldiers who beat us to pulp
and did their other tricks on us are going to have to go on living in
this society with the children of the other side. That's tomorrow's
world and I don't want that world to come to be wounded and
damaged by the mistakes of the past. It's not that I want to sweeten
the mistakes of the past but I think there are things that nobody can
restore to you and cannot be compensated, even though there are
people who think they can be. There are things involving one's way
of thinking that are not really open to discussion. Do you know what
it's like to have an old man of seventy or eighty rotting in jail? I don't
want to be the executioner of those who were my executioners . . .
I'm a bit of a softy precisely because I wore a forty-five on my belt.
I fought for social change, not to present my bill to so-and-so or
such-and-such. What's more, some of the victims might have been
white peace doves, but others weren't, it was Fatherland or Death
for them. We were the ones who shouted "Execute the bastard".
Come off it, we weren't babes on the breast, so don't come on like
Little Red Riding Hood with me now.' There are arguments here
worth serious consideration, but at no point does Mujica recognise
the need or the right that the whole population has to know the truth
about what happened, about who did what to whom, and where the
'disappeared' still unaccounted for ended up. It is possible to
renounce the desire for justice but the historical truth belongs to all,
not just to those involved, and nowhere that I have found does
Mujica square up to this issue.

Yet the biggest failures or defeats of Mujica's presidency remain
the fields of public service and public education. With regard to the
first, the much cherished job security gave it what he termed an 'aris-
tocratic tinge that was antidemocratic (why should it only be
available to some and not others?)' as well as inducing a culture
recognised by every Uruguayan that basically says that the purpose
of the public service is not to serve the public but to guarantee jobs
and pensions for the employees. So, while competitive contracts
could be introduced at the higher administrative levels, the most the
unions could be persuaded to do at lower and middle levels is some
productivity efficiencies that made a noticeable difference in some
sectors, as did decent salary increases; but unions quite simply
distrusted any proposals of wholesale restructuring so plans for

major reforms, as on so many previous occasions, had to be shelved. Similar or analogous results were obtained in the tax sector, because all attempts at progressive taxes on salaries were met with the unmoveable belief that it was a fundamental right of the worker not to pay tax as far as humanly possible. Uruguayan unions and their members have never been persuaded that a tax system that relies for well over half its revenue on indirect taxes on the sale of goods and the provision of services instead of on the graded taxation of salaries is in fact more prejudicial to the less well paid.

On education, the international PISA tests that examine students' basic skills showed a consistent decline for Uruguayan public school pupils. Rhetorical sleights of hand that tried to show how the tests themselves were prejudicial only increased the general population's rancour, although the policy of including all in the non-selective public sphere, especially where the newly targeted poor were concerned, would greatly increase the numbers of those who had no familiarity with school, its demands or frequency, a factor that would affect average scores in any survey. Mujica did not want any kind of competition between schools but he did want 'the schools Head and the staff to have some considerable freedom of movement in taking the school forward, and if a particular school excels, then all can learn from it. But there's a public employee mentality that says things must be this way, everything flat, equal. Well, that battle is still to be fought but what will happen, I can't say. But for me it's a subject still pending.'

Perhaps the last word on his government should be Mujica's own, here from January 2013 with still two years to go: 'Some shameful things that have been dragging on for many years are still with us but have been severely reduced. Indigence and poverty have not been rubbed out, but we have been able to maintain a policy of redistribution, and that's our best achievement, perhaps. The area where most is still lacking? Education is the issue where little got done and most is still to do. We got the University of Technology through, though not the plan we would have preferred, and we have to start from zero. But in secondary education we have a huge debt . . . We are stuck in an old French paradigm abandoned in France forty years ago, and you can see in secondary school the weakening of social ties. Mothers turn up angry and demanding whereas before teachers had the tacit support of the kids' families . . . Only now have we got back to where we were in the 1960s. We've had 50 years of useless history . . . the Uruguay of my youth had more or less the level of redistribution that we have just managed to get back to.'

Since leaving office Mujica, as he always promised, has continued his work as active militant both at home and abroad. He actively supported his wife's unsuccessful campaign to become Mayor of Montevideo in early 2015, has represented the MPP, his sector of the Broad Front, in the Senate, alongside his wife, while the two of them have travelled widely around the world, as Mujica has responded to invitations to give guest lectures or participate in the launching of translations of books about him. On this latter front, during November 2015 he received what must be an unusual honour for an ex-president of any country on the planet: *Brecha*, Uruguay's leading independent left weekly, devoted an entire back cover to books in Japanese about him!

On a more serious note, in late October 2015 Mujica and Lucía Topolansky announced their intention of leaving parliament in April 2016. Conspiracy theorists immediately concluded that this was to give Mujica time to plan a second shot at the Presidency in 2019 and, as he threatened on 1 March 2015, receive back from Tabaré Vázquez that presidential sash, if only to then resign so the real candidate, who would have been the running mate for purposes of election, could step into an office he or she would have had less chance of reaching on their own devices. This sounds too Machiavellian for a specialist in improvised tactics. It is, I think, far more likely that what Mujica has said is the simple truth: biology has caught up with both of them, and they want to give the MPP ample time before 2019 to find and prepare younger members to replace them as sector leaders and Senate ticket front runners. However, as not just a few Uruguayans have recently noticed, Mujica looks younger these days every time he appears on television . . .

Conclusion

A Left Alternative?

Who shot Lenin? An anarchist. The Left is always going to generate
an Ultra-Left that unintentionally ends up doing the Right a favour.
JOSÉ 'PEPE' MUJICA

The epigraph to this Conclusion contains a reminder about – and perhaps to – Mujica himself and those of his former guerrilla comrades who abandoned the MLN in its democratic phase to continue sniping from the sidelines in the name of what was being left behind. What the quotation foregrounds is the already mentioned dilemma those on the left face when forced to operate in a political environment hostile to them: how far to go in participating and cooperating with it and when to call an analytical and critical halt to this process because inviolable principles have somehow been compromised or forgotten. The more moderate among the groups comprising the Broad Front see Mujica and Lucía Topolansky themselves and their MPP as an 'ultra-left' that might undo the Front's popularity among the general population. The position can also be that of militant trade union leaders whose calls for strike action risk undermining the very progressive government their members' votes helped get into power. Put another way perhaps more suited to Mujica with his anarchist inclinations, it's a matter of finding the line separating what one can learn from reading the history of the 1871 Paris commune and a nostalgic desire to somehow reproduce it starting in Liberty Square in Montevideo today, and how the advocacy of the second can impede the implementation in current circumstances of what might be genuinely possible for those who do the first. What follows consists largely of sometimes lengthy extracts, with some brief commentary, from Mujica's speeches and interviews between his presidential campaign in 2009 and the later period of his presidency that ended formally on March 1, 2015. Readers will have to judge for themselves how he succeeds or fails in negotiating this line between the provocative and the useful on the one hand, and the merely eccentric or whimsical on the other, as he becomes at times almost messianically aware of his growing ability to exploit the globalised electronic technologies he both welcomes and questions to reach a planet-wide audience about matters that he knows may have planetary significance.

The Philosopher takes Power while the Politician Thinks

In a September 2013 interview Mujica made a revealing disclosure about what guides his improvisation abilities when making his often effective and memorable presentations: 'I'm not Machiavellian about it, far from it, but I've got a way of putting things that's different, that works like a hook with bait. I could begin to explain the economy, but they'd all get up and leave. I throw them a juicy morsel and they're hooked. It's different; more than the content, it's the form. Tolstoy [had a character say] in the *Kreutzer Sonata*: "If I'd met my wife wearing a barrel, I'd never have fallen in love with her". The form becomes part of the content, as I learnt from Don José Bergamín in his classes on literary composition. It's not a question of form and content; the form is part of the content.' Mujica had coaches and minders during his campaigns, but it is instructive that what he finds most useful in describing how he talks politics or philosophy comes from a university tutorial on a topic in a specialist high art category: literary composition. It is a timely riposte to those classically and privately educated elitists who see Mujica as a cultural bull in a china shop, a crass and vulgar autodidact whose knowledge is often second-hand or half-digested. While he may not want a society of humanities specialists in a nation that so much needs to appreciate and exploit scientific knowledge, Mujica is not blithely dismissive of the attractions and usefulness of the arts and literature. He would just want such minority interests to be the prerogative of us all, as far as is possible.

As though to underline his approach as well as to curry support from a sector sympathetic to him, on 29 April 2009, during the campaign, Mujica invited intellectuals, writers and other cultural workers to a lecture theatre in Parliament. His speech frequently seems to co-opt in almost utilitarian fashion all cultural forms and their practitioners into some form of teaching, although the references to the pleasures of culture remind us of his own memory of a former girlfriend long gone who left him, however, with a permanent love of classical music that he had never heard until she came along. For Mujica, **Culture** is not only didactic, as important as that may be, but what was available to him by chance must now be part of planned policy:

'I like to think of myself as someone who likes bathing in pools filled with the intelligence, culture and wisdom of others. The more other, the better. The more it doesn't coincide with my own little knowledge, the better. The weekly *Búsqueda* [*Search*] has a beautiful sentence it uses as its emblem: "I do not say what I say as a knowledgeable man but as someone searching alongside you". For once I agree with *Búsqueda* [a right-wing liberal publication whose journalists frequently interviewed Mujica during his presidency]. But how much I agree with that! And I say what I say not as some know-all farmer, not as some well-read peasant, but as someone searching alongside you. I say it while searching because only the ignorant believe the truth to be definitive and robust, while really it is but provisional and slippery. We have to search it out because it runs from hiding place to hiding place.'

'The intelligence that helps a country is distributed intelligence, that which is not only in laboratories or universities but that which walks along the street. There used to be a saying: "Don't give a boy a fish to eat; teach him to fish". Today we ought to say: "Don't give children bits of information; teach them to think", because the way things are going, the depositories of information are no longer going to be in our heads but out there, accessible for searching on the Internet. That's where all information, all data, everything that is known, is going to be. In other words, stored there will be all the answers. What will not be there are all the questions. The real issue, then, is going to be our capacity to ask the right questions, our capacity to formulate fertile questions, those which set off new kinds of research and learning.'

'We need to "massify" intelligence, first to make ourselves more powerful producers, which in itself may be a matter of our very survival. But this life is about enjoyment as well as production. And you [cultural and intellectual workers] know better than anyone that knowledge and culture are not only effort but pleasure, too . . . How good it would be if these tasty morsels were part of the quality of life Uruguay could offer all its people, if there were large quantities of intellectual food everywhere. Not because it would be elegant but because it would be enjoyable.'

'I said before that the intelligence that serves a country best is distributed intelligence. Now I would like to add that the kind of dissatisfaction ['inconformismo' in Mujica's Spanish] that serves a country best is distributed dissatisfaction, the disquiet that has invaded all our daily lives and pushes us to ask ourselves whether we could not be doing better what ever it is we do. This kind of dissatisfaction is in the very nature of what you cultural workers do, but we need it to become second nature to all of us . . . because everything, literally everything, can be done a bit better today than it was done yesterday; everything, from making a bed to making an integrated circuit. We need an epidemic of non-conformism, and that too is cultural, because it irradiates out from the intellectual and cultural centres to the margins of society.'

'Friends, the bridge between this today and that tomorrow we all want has a name and that name is education but this bridge is long and difficult to cross. Because one thing is the rhetoric of education and quite another is the decision we all take to make the sacrifice implied in launching a huge effort in education and in sustaining it over time. The returns on investment in education are slow and no government sees them all, so they arouse resistance as they demand the postponement of other projects. However, we must do it; we owe it to our children and grand-children, and we must do it know while the new computer and Internet technologies are still fresh and our opening vistas for knowledge never seen in human history before now . . . I feel like those humans who saw a wheel or fire for the first time. It feels like we are experiencing a milestone in human history. The doors of all the museums and all the libraries are opening up; all the scientific journals and all the world's books are going to be accessible to all. And probably all films and all music, too. We need every Uruguayan to be able to swim in this torrent, to dive into this current and swim in it like a fish in water . . . Full-time schools, university faculties in the interior, and English from kindergarten in state schools, not because the Americans speak it, but because it's the language with which even the Chinese communicate with the rest of the world. We can't afford to be left out, we can't afford to leave our kids out. These are the instruments that allow us to interact with the universal knowledge explosion which will not simplify our lives but make them more complicated. They oblige us to go further and deeper in education; there is no greater task before us.'

'Election time is a blessing and a curse. A curse because it sets us squabbling and running races against each other. A blessing because it allows us to live together in a civilised way. A double blessing because with all their imperfections, elections allow us to choose our own destiny. And we have all learnt that the worse democracy is preferable to the best dictatorship . . . Those of us who work here in Parliament do so to be of service, NOT to serve ourselves off the State.'

At the 'Rio + 20' Summit in Rio de Janeiro on 20 June 2012, Mujica made the first of his speeches that brought him attention across the world. In an improvised address after listening for two days to all sorts of environmental warnings and homilies, he was irritated just enough to remind all the conferees that the real issue they should be concerned about was not global warming and melting icebergs, but **Global Politics**:

'Are we governing globalisation or is globalisation governing us? Can we talk about solidarity and all of us being together in an economy based on unbridled competition? How far does our fraternity really stretch? I'm not saying this to deny the importance of this event. Quite the contrary: the challenge we face is colossal but the really great crisis is not ecological but political . . . we cannot go on indefinitely being governed by the market; rather, we must govern the market. That's why I say that, in my humble opinion, the problem we have is of a political nature. The ancient philosophers – Epicurus, Seneca as well as the Aymara Indians – defined as poor not the person who has little but the person who needs an infinite amount and desires ever more . . . We must realise that the drinking water crisis and the attacks on the environment are not the cause. The cause is the civilisation model we have constructed. What we need to revise is our way of life . . . My worker comrades struggled hard to get the 8-hour working day. Now they can make it six hours. But the guy who works only six hours needs two jobs, so he's working more than before. Why? To pay all the monthly bills and repayments, and before he knows it, he's an old rheumatic like me and his life's gone by . . . and you have to ask, is that the point of human life? These things I'm saying are elementary, there can be no development that opposes human happiness, because the most important treasure we have is happiness. When we fight for the environment we need to remember that the prime element in our environment is called human happiness.'

An interview in the Montevideo weekly *Brecha* on January 4, 2013, reminds us that the Mujica on the smaller Uruguayan national stage is no less relevant to us than the more self-consciously international figure as he speaks about his **Socialist Vision**:

'I've been putting about 8,000 US dollars of my salary every month into the Plan Juntos [the self-help social housing program Mujica founded] for ages . . . Do you think there's anybody else in the government who puts in even 50 cents? No. I had to put up a sign on my office door which says, "Don't shame your President; pay your dues to the Broad Front". It's there to remind our bureaucrats to pay their contributions to the Front. They've got two nice houses and another in some seaside resort while half Uruguay still needs decent housing, right? But I can't impose anything on them. Why not? Because the pressures of the society we live in are stronger. People say that Pepe is right about consumerism, they applaud me, but they don't take any notice (Mujica says laughing).'

'I have a socialist vision and I'm super-critical of capitalism. I struggle to go beyond it but it's not a solution that's just round the corner [in Spanish 'a la vuelta de la esquina', a reminder of a commonplace of revolutionary thinking in the 1960s, and the title of one of the best Uruguayan books written about it]. To jump from a backward society straight to socialism was a fantasy from another time. I don't believe in the dictatorship of the proletariat either, another fairy story we swallowed. The construction of socialism cannot be at loggerheads with freedom. I might shade some details here and there on this but I'm not swallowing the capitalist pill, no way . . . Sweden and Norway are closer to socialism than we are [because they have developed further their forces of production]. But this doesn't mean that getting richer and having greater knowledge development gets you straight to socialism. No, then there's the politics.'

'Presidents are always alone. For various reasons, I don't feel alone on the street. On the contrary, I feel there's almost too much company, because they sort of besiege me. I understand political construction to be a collective enterprise and there ought to be important collective forums where you can discuss things as equals. So when I say lonely that's what I'm referring to because I don't have a central committee to talk things through with. I've got only a Council of Ministers. That's why I'm against re-election. Once presidents get into power, they generate a circle of people round them that should not be left there too long.' *Elsewhere in the same year (2013) Mujica expanded on the same topic:* 'I'm very republican. The great defect of the semi-populist formulas is that indirectly they're somewhat Caesarist; they end up leaving behind a court and those around it. It's an anti-republican category within society, a new kind of nobility. It's the most dangerous thing about [really strong leaders]. They are less dangerous in themselves than for the people surrounding them.'

'I am austere, not poor, and I don't defend any kind of "poorism". What I advocate is living light on luggage, so I don't get so attached to things I no longer have time to do what I want. I live as I think, so I'm weird. People accept me as weird, but they're not going to follow my example.'

It is worth recalling at this point a MLN–Tupamaros document from 1972 that allows us to see what there still is in Mujica's thinking here that can be directly related to his guerrilla warrior past as well as allowing us to see how far he has travelled away from it: 'The leadership organisms are collegiate; there are no "sacred cows". The risks and the penury are the same for all. Leaders go into action; we don't want any pure theorists. We aspire to the proletarianisation of all militants through a high quota of manual work, ideological work, the preaching and practice of austerity. We aim to avoid the distortions of urban guerrilla warfare, neutralise the noxious effects of petit-bourgeois and middle-class individualism that our recruits often bring with them, form the "new man" and increase our confidence in each other. Even the bourgeois press has had to acknowledge this austerity.'

A March 2013 interview in the Montevideo monthly, *Lento*, expands on Mujica's views a couple of months earlier, offering along the way what might be a gloss on his own words quoted above as the heading to this Conclusion:

'The 1930s and 40s was a time when there reigned on the left a kind of economic automatism: capitalism, through its own contradictions, would lead unequivocally to socialism, and that seemed to be the paradigm of evolution, a predetermined road. That might look ridiculous today, but it was the ABC of a significant part of the world socialist movement. But the fall of capitalism was not automatic because it showed an enormous capacity to recycle itself permanently and live in crisis. Secondly, it became clear that nobody could say they know where the key to all this lies. Looking back at it over time gives food for thought, and the Sweden of Olof Palme was closer to socialism than what we saw elsewhere. One has to have the intellectual honesty to admit this even though it hurts. Then it becomes necessary to revalue things that were undervalued, like the vicissitudes of human life. Was it worth sacrificing the lives of one, two, three generations for a utopia whose nature we thought we could confidently predict? And why do I sacrifice people's present? It's a moral problem we should set ourselves with respect to what can and cannot be done . . . I'd include the Tupamaros in that: we too were prisoners of an epoch and a time. Those schemes were out there. Everything was solved by taking power and building society up, as though it were a work of craftsmanship. But things weren't so simple. Human beings are more complicated. Not that I renounce all that; it would be like renouncing love. What I renounce is everyone staying stuck there like fossils after what happened, seeing the Soviet Union collapse without a shot. And I'm supposed to go on following the analyses of Lenin? There's the problem: on the left there are conservative attitudes that look as if they are sustaining left-wing positions that actually turn into reactionary ones. You don't learn a thing from reality if you can't acquire a critical vision of all that and start looking at it in a more complex way. I understand that if one were to say "socialism is impossible, a heap of crap; capitalism is the high point of human history", OK, that's it, you've changed sides, you've abdicated. Capitalism may be many things, but it has a damned enormous creative force and you've got to respect it for that. We have to use it, but also get beyond it.'

Similarly but more dramatically, we find the following in the weekly *Voces* for 12 September 2013, where Sendic's idea of an even broader front seems to be recycled:

'The socialist bloc didn't leave even the poetry of the odd shot. It fell like a rotten tree. It's shameful. Something that cost so much sacrifice, that presumed the commitment of masses and militants in their thousands. The millions sacrificed in the Second World War. To have something capable of beating the Nazi axis fall like a worm-ridden log is a shameful thing . . . [In Uruguay] there's a root problem, I think, and we have to go [further than just a few more little reforms here and there]. What is the way forward? I don't know, I don't have it clear in my head, but let me try. Let me experiment and change the roots of the State. This is part of the left's struggle; it's the left's dilemma. I don't want to make the separation between social democrats and revolutionaries because then we get roast on the spit and end up working for the right. No, social democrats and revolutionaries, all more or less crazy and mixed in together, right? Because there's a bigger picture, a left sensibility toward social differences, which we might call the progressive world. Even just trying to distribute the fiscal load in ways fairer to the weakest, people start to live better. Does it change the system? No, it doesn't change the system, but life's short and in the meantime we can improve things for people. As I've already said, I don't buy this stuff about sacrificing one or two generations so that others can come after who don't even remember what happened but can throw caution to the winds. No. Stick with today, and have people live the best way possible and make sure the most left behind are at last the first to be remembered.'

At this point I would like, as I did at corresponding moments earlier in this book, to quote Alain Badiou, not because of some easy correspondence between his thinking and Mujica's but as two perhaps parallel alternatives in the current climate of resurgence in left-wing thinking. Here, both short passages are taken from

Badiou's *Ethics: An Essay on the Understanding of Evil*: 'To be sure, the enemy, comforted by the collapse of authoritarian socialism, dominates everywhere. But it is also true that we are entering a long period of recomposition, both for emancipatory political thought and for those effective practical forces that correspond to it'; 'The celebrated "end of ideologies" heralded everywhere as the good news which opens the way for the "return of ethics" signifies in fact the espousal of the twistings and turnings of necessity, and an extraordinary impoverishment of the active, militant value of principles.' In effect, Badiou seeks to develop a new philosophy of political emancipation out of the ruins of the deviations of Marxist thinking that produced so-called 'existing socialism', while Mujica's practice as militant and politician illustrate the forms such a philosophy might take in practice.

At the United Nations on 24 September 2013, Mujica gave the speech that has guaranteed his worldwide fame. At the same time it is a kind of messianic *summum* of his thinking and in some ways perhaps implies he is more a Tupamaro than ever, except that instead of dynamiting only the Uruguayan state, he would if he could dismantle the entire United Nations organisation and rebuild it from the ground up with his developing world comrades. It is an excoriating **World View**:

'I am from the South, I come from the South, on the corner where Atlantic Ocean meets River Plate. My country is a gently undulating plain, temperate of climate and full of livestock. Its history is made up of ports, leather, corned beef, wool and meat. It had purple decades of horse and lance until at last, at the start of the twentieth century, it became a vanguard in matters of society, state and education. Indeed, I would go so far as to say that social democracy was invented in Uruguay. For nearly fifty years the world saw us as a Switzerland, while really we were a bastard offshoot of the British Empire, and when it fell we "lived" the bitter honey of funereal exchange, we stagnated and yearned for the past. We spent fifty years remembering Maracaná [the name of the Rio de Janeiro stadium where Uruguay beat Brazil in the final of the 1950 Soccer World Cup, a David and Goliath story that is a point of reference in the history and culture of both nations] almost without growing. Today we have reappeared in this globalised world, still learning from our suffering. My own story is that of a young man who, like so many others, wanted to change his epoch and his world by following the libertarian dream of a classless society. My mistakes are children of their time. I assume responsibility for them but there are times when I cry out still: "Oh for the strength we had when we believed so much Utopia was just over the horizon". However, I don't live looking back because today's reality was born out of yesterday's fertile ashes. Neither do I live just to settle accounts or to hear the echo of my memories. I fret about the future I will not see but which is also the measure of my commitment. A world with better human beings remains possible, but right now humanity's first task is maybe just to survive.'

'I am from the South and from the South I come to this assembly. I come burdened with the load of millions of poor compatriots from the cities, plains, jungles, pampas and tunnels of Latin America, a single Commonwealth of Nations that has to take on our obliterated original cultures, the remains of colonialism in the Malvinas/Falklands, the sad and useless blockade of Cuba, and electronic surveillance in countries like Brazil that is the child of poisonous mistrust. I come laden with a huge social debt, with the need to defend Amazonia, the seas and our great rivers. I bear the duty to fight for a Fatherland for All and for peace in Colombia, for tolerance and respect toward those who are different, and for the obligation never to intervene against the will of others.'

'We promise a life of waste and squander, which is a countdown against the natural environment and against the future of humanity. A civilization against simplicity, against sobriety, against all natural cycles, and worse still, a civilization against the freedom that supposes time to experience human relations, love, friendship, adventure, solidarity, family. A civilization against time you don't pay for but can use to enjoy the beauty of the natural world. We demolish natural forests only to replace them with anonymous asphalt jungles. We fight sedentary lives with walking machines in gyms, insomnia with sleeping pills, loneliness with electronics . . . The guy on the street of our time wanders between finance companies and the acclimatised tedium of air-conditioned office routine, always dreaming of holidays and freedom, of finally closing all accounts, until one day the heart stops and it's thank you and good night.'

'We can't manage globalisation because our thinking is not global, but we don't know if this is a cultural limitation or a biological frontier. Our epoch is portentously revolutionary like no other earlier period in human history, but with no self-aware or even instinctive sense of leadership. Even less some kind of organised political leadership because in this matter we have no philosophical precursors of importance. The ambition that fired material, technical and scientific progress is paradoxically now drawing us toward a misty abyss. An epoch without history, and we have neither eyes nor collective intelligence to go on colonizing and transforming ourselves. It seems as though objects have assumed autonomy and are subjugating humans. On every side we see glimpses of the way forward but it is impossible to collectivise major decisions for the whole. Individual ambition triumphs over the higher ambition of the species. Let's be clear: what do I mean by "the whole"? The global life of System Earth, including human life with all its fragile equilibrium that makes it possible for us to reproduce ourselves and continue on.'

'On the other side are republics that arose to affirm that all humans are equal, that nobody is more than anybody else, and whose governments should represent the common good, justice and equality. They often stray and are forgotten by ordinary people, but republics were not built to vegetate on top of the mass but are on the contrary a functional part of it and therefore owe their existence to majorities.'

'Through feudal memories or class domination or consumerist culture, republics and their leaderships adopt a "splendiferous" daily life style that excludes the actions of the common people who live and dream and should be the central recipient of their services. Governments should be like the common republicans who make up the people.

'We are wont to cultivate feudal archaisms, self-indulgent courtesies, hierarchical differences, that have sapped the best out of our republics. The play of these and other factors keeps us in prehistory and today it is still impossible to renounce war when politics fails. So the economy is strangled and we waste resources. Every minute two million dollars are spent on military budgets while medical research on the whole planet barely consumes a fifth of what is spent on military research and development. This process ensures the continuation of hatred and fanaticism, the sources of new wars that also cost fortunes . . . The United Nations Organisation languishes and becomes bureaucratised through lack of power and autonomy, above all through its lack of democracy with respect to the weaker parts of the world that are the majority. Just as one example, Uruguayans participate with between thirteen and fifteen per cent of our armed forces in the UN peace missions. We have been doing this for years, always in the spots assigned to us, but in the places where decisions are made and resources allotted, we're not even there to serve the coffee. [In 2016 Uruguay will play a role as rotating Chair of the UN Security Council] In the deepest part of our hearts there resides a longing to help humankind leave prehistory and file away war as a recourse when politics fails, for in my solitude I have known what war is . . . But these dreams imply a struggle for an agenda of global agreements that begin to govern our history and overcome the threats to life. The species needs a government for the whole of humanity that exceeds individualism and works to create political brains that refer to science and knowledge rather than short-term interests. This is neither easy *nor rapid, even supposing it to be possible.' Here Mujica seems to be envisaging the United Nations as, in effect, his own Movement for Popular Participation writ large.*

Mujica was in Santiago de Cuba in July 2013 for the sixtieth anniversary of Fidel Castro's failed assault on the Moncada barracks, which Mujica called a 'temple', on 26 July 1953. It took no little courage on his part, amid the praise he heaped on revolutionary Cuba as an example for all Latin Americans, to either explicitly say or quite directly imply that they got it wrong, that the premises the Cubans had used and that others, including the MLN, had learnt from, were in fact mistaken. It is worth watching the video of Mujica giving the speech on YouTube to see the invited Cuban and international audience at first uncomfortable and quite bemused over where he is going with what at first might be taken as counter-revolutionary innuendo, followed by the relief as the message became clear to them, and the standing ovation he received at the close. The reference to learning from failure and the cost of the impossible is to the apparent paradox of a triumphant revolution using a past defeat as the occasion of its country's national day, while the idea of 'going forward finding roads as we go' recalls the MLN's own notion, borrowed in part from the theorisation of the Cuban experience, that 'revolutionary situations are created by revolutionary actions.' Mujica's emphasis on respect and tolerance for the different may be taken as pointed references to both Cuba and the USA and to relations between the two as well as discrimination of one sort or another in each of them, while the final sentence suggests that in Cuba, too, despite its revolutionary achievements and credentials since the reversal of the 1953 failed attack all are gathered in Santiago to commemorate, military 'barracks' retain their conventional 'prehistoric' functions because of the fear that armed conflict remains the only alternative when politics and diplomacy fail. For Mujica, only cultural change through education can change this state of affairs:

'Social change does not have a laboratory in which you can experiment scientifically first. Social change *is* the experiment constructed by the people through struggle. And we men and women walk forward finding roads as we go, recreating and learning from our own experience, from the road of suffering, from our failures, how to get back on our feet again and again. Social change is not just round the corner. Quite simply, social change is not right there, within arm's reach. It's a long collective exercise in construction, the product of effort, work, errors, successes, commitment and sacrifice. It's always been like that. The impossible costs a little more, it seems. But for that reason, in the end there are no defeats, for the only defeats are those endured by people who give up the fight.'

'For Latin Americans the Cuban Revolution is the revolution of dignity and self-esteem . . . It sowed dreams in us, it turned us into Don Quixotes, we dreamed that in fifteen or twenty years we could create a totally different society. But we crashed into history. Material changes are much easier than cultural ones. But cultural changes are definitely the real cement of history, and are a slow sowing over many generations . . . The world is only possible if it respects diversity. The world and the future are only possible if we accustom ourselves to understanding that the world is diversity and respect, dignity and tolerance, and that nobody has the right to be great and strong if it means treading all over the weak . . . The word revolution acquires a universal meaning when the world is globalised' and becomes 'the struggle to make the world a better place.'

'Humanity will leave prehistory only when all barracks have become schools and universities.' It is worth confronting this conclusion with the following assertion, once again from Alain Badiou, this time from an essay on 'Philosophy and the "War against Terror"' collected in his *Polemics*: 'For, ever since Aeschylus's *Oresteia*, so for a long time, we've known that the question is to know how to replace violence with justice.' *But you need to be in school or university rather than in the army to learn that.*

In February 2014, Mujica's speech to the Second Summit of the Community of Latin American and Caribbean Nations gathered up ideas that he had already adumbrated in his celebrated earlier United Nations speech cited above, but such recycling is an inevitable part of improvisation as well as of propaganda:

'History is like a kitbag on your back, it's the only real thing we can half-see. The future is always uncertain, but is our desire, our preoccupation, our challenge.'

'If humanity is incapable of thinking as a species, if humanity continues to think nationally or only in terms of social class, thinking only about what are narrowly our own affairs, civilization is doomed . . . Globalisation is a fact, a fact that is leading us to catastrophe, if we are not able to give backbone to a program of self-awareness and conscience.'

'I believe humanity must fight for its real happiness, which is to have time to live. To be free one must have time, a bit of time, to live, to be able to cultivate the three, four or five things that are inevitably, necessarily linked to life; after that, all the rest is rush and sorrow. However, for the majorities to have this time, we have to look after natural resources, we have to take care of politics and its image . . . We have to dress like English gentlemen because that is the suit industrialisation imposed on the world. Even the Japanese had to set aside the kimono to be taken seriously in the world, and we all had to dress up like monkeys with ties round their necks.' We can add that Mujica has never worn a suit and tie since he needed to wear one on an MLN guerrilla operation!

'It's absolutely clear to me that you don't redistribute poverty, and nothing on this planet has proved to be as strong and creative as capitalist economy, which has revolutionised humanity with its technology and science but has also signalled the growth in our culture of selfishness and the loss of fraternity among communities. It's not easy to repair this, comrades, it's going to be a long struggle. There's no solution just round the corner, there's no magic transformation just round the corner, and history is not changed by congress declarations. We have to create an enormous foundation of confidence in our peoples, and that means a long struggle on all fronts. In my humble opinion, the worst crisis facing humanity is political. Ours is a civilisation that charges ahead and takes us with it by the nose, and we don't control it. The ever-growing demands of the market are stronger than we are, and we confuse the need to consume to live with covering up the need to squander resources, energy, and nothing can rationalise this.'

'Life is not long enough to do all there is to do. If we can't create political currents, intelligent thinking, if we can't set the challenge to the Latin American intellectual community, if we can't sow seed in the heads of future generations, we will be just the observers of our own future misfortunes, and we'll complain and spend our lives trying to repair what we can. And I'm afraid that one of the misfortunes of modern politics is to have abandoned the field of philosophy and become too much an economic prescription pad. It's not that economics is unimportant but humanity doesn't ask itself questions like "Where are we going?", "What kind of future do we want?", "What is our responsibility for life itself?" Human life is almost a miracle in the enormous mineral silence of the universe, almost a miracle! This near-miracle on our planet deserves human beings gifted with a conscience and a self-awareness who spend most of their energy on defending the parameters of life for the generations still to come. That's why those of us from the "young continent" must join together. Thank you.'

A year later in February 2015, Mujica's last official speech as President before handing over power to Tabaré Vázquez on March 1 was to the Third Summit of the same Community of Latin American and Caribbean Nations. Mujica's speech, over-long and less controlled than usual, largely repeated what he had said the year before. This paragraph is a summary with quotations of its more elegiac and valedictory moments:

Even if Uruguay had less social and economic inequality than many other LA countries, Mujica still felt 'sorrow' that at the end of his term, 0.5% of his country's 3,300,000 people were indigent and some 10% were below the poverty line. And if 30% of Latin America as a whole was in that position, it was about time its inhabitants stopped 'sending the bill to US imperialism or European high-handedness, because that is just the way they are; in the end it's our lack of skill and our inability to agree among ourselves' that stops Latin America progressing faster. He repeated the same line on capitalism, emphasising its contradictory nature: 'capable of generating great wealth but with enormous moral poverty in its intestines'. He wanted 'to stick his neck out in support of politics with a capital "P": there's one thing that has no price and no substitute: you shouldn't enter mainstream politics to make business deals or to live better but to commit oneself with affection to the cause of the people' because 'in the long process of transforming society you need collective construction and an ethics of commitment.'

I once again call on Alain Badiou, here from his *The Rebirth of History: Times of Riots and Uprisings*: 'If there is to be a rebirth of History, it will not come from the barbaric conservatism of capitalism and the determination of all state apparatuses to maintain its demented pattern. The only possible reawakening is the popular initiative in which the power of an Idea will take root.' Everything indicates Mujica would agree with the main thrust of these statements, even if he would then have to invite Badiou to sit down and negotiate the exact meaning of 'Idea' with a capital 'I'. As he told a Broad Front seminar on "The Left of the Future" just one day before handing over the presidential sash: 'We can only go forward if we do it as a collective and our pace is that of the slowest and not of some vanguard up front.'

What is Left?

'One thing I'm going to leave behind [Mujica said in a September 2013 interview] is a genuinely republican presidency that burns a mark in the way society categorises it, a confrontation with the nobility, with those who are into wigs and ornament, all that stuff. I believe essentially in a world of equality for all that is different but for several reasons a set of medieval institutions have managed to sneak in: the red carpet, the guys who blow horns when someone enters the castle and all the serving staff have to line up. All that liturgy and paraphernalia accepted in the free play of democracy. You arrive someplace, you go down the steps and they play something for you and you've arrived needing to go to the bathroom but you've got to hold it in. Why are you supposed to make those poor people stand like stakes for two hours to honour an old bloke from God knows where? Come off it! Either we're equal or we're not. What's all of it for? . . . I defend humanity, humanity as it is and that you have to accept as it is. And the president is an equal to whom we give certain responsibilities, that's all. Suddenly he's an angry old fool who talks rubbish but at least he's flesh and blood like the rest of us . . . you shouldn't bow before human beings or apostrophize them either. They can't touch the sky with their hands nor are they gods and, besides, they're temporary, they pass on. I'm going to go down in the comic strip history ['historieta'] of the nation as a transgressor of the image and I won't be forgiven . . . Structural change in any society is easier than cultural change. Culture is the slowest thing to change and it gets out of phase with the rest. Material reality changes but you've still got the pre-eminence of a culture from the past that no longer fits with material reality, you see it every day.'

For Mujica, everything associated with the exercise of power is provisional, transitory and circumstantial, presidents as well as constitutions, because they are all dependent on the histories, personal and collective, and the social and ideological forces that converge at the particular moment and site of their appearance. As he said when his proposed road and school tax on large rural properties was declared unconstitutional: 'We've got a constitution made by and for landowners'. It is on account of this that the paraphernalia and trappings associated with wealth and the exercise of power seem to Mujica both pathetic and pointless, since they only appear to disguise what is for him a perfectly acceptable and simple truth that many seek to hide under a veil of self-importance. No human and nothing made by humans stands outside history or the laws of thermodynamics, but that is also what makes them subject to change and human agency, which is in turn what, for Mujica, makes paramount the politics of individual and class emancipation.

On 27 February 2015, in his farewell 'Message to the Uruguayan People' on standing down as President, which he admitted to have written out in full, a method very unusual for him, he summarised his story:

'Meanwhile, the entire world was sinking into a Cold War, a struggle between a plutocracy with flags of democracy and a bureaucracy with socialist flags. They were years of stagnation, of militant utopia. We ended up gambling everything, like many others. We suffered and caused suffering to others and we are aware of it. We paid an enormous price, but miraculously we remain alive, tempered and learning from adversity. I have reconceptualised my whole life as dedication and a value worth fighting for above all else and, more humble and more republican, the idea that nobody is better than anybody else is more ingrained in me than ever.'

Mujica then continued with a paragraph that, with few minor changes, would not have been out of place in an MLN document from the 1960s or in one of the many published interviews at the time with some anonymous Tupamaro clandestine warrior: 'Sober, with little baggage, so as to have more free time to use socially through my existence, because this is my way of happiness after so much coming and going, I learnt that the only battle lost is that which is abandoned and moreover, dear people, that there is no final destination but the road itself and that many others will make their contribution and continue on that road of struggle. Five years have passed in a struggle between the natural selfishness we carry within us put there by nature so we can defend our lives and those of the family nucleus that surrounds us and that other great force, solidarity. Let's be clear that solidarity is the long-term defence of the species, while egoism is needed as an instrument to defend our lives and those of our loved ones.'

Finally, an emotional 'Until we meet again' that confirms at the very close that, for Mujica, the politics of a people's nationalism is life itself: 'Dear people, thank you for your hugs and embraces. Thank you for your criticism, your affection and your profound fraternal fellowship in the lonely moments during my Presidency. If I had two lives, I would spend all of both helping in your struggles, because it is the most splendid way of loving life I have been able to find in all my nearly eighty years. I'm not leaving; I'm arriving. I will go only with my last breath and wherever I am, I shall be at your side, I shall be with you, because that is the better way of being on the side of life. Thank you, beloved people.'

In case we might think he had here given in to his own sense of self-importance, we should remind ourselves of the words quoted earlier from an interview in March 2005:

'I don't want to be remembered. If I could choose, what I want is to be forgotten. There's nothing worse than nostalgia, to go around believing in dead gods. You have to bury the dead and honour them once a year, on the right day . . . you can't build anything with the dead. People need to live boldly, looking to the front. One has to serve as fertiliser, not as an obstacle. And serving as fertiliser means mineralising oneself, simplifying oneself, so as to become something useful.' *Observation of nature and his reading about it only confirm for Mujica that individual members of species count for very little and only then as fragments of a whole, an atheistic – or perhaps, in his case, pantheistic – conviction that is at the root of his collectivist politics and of the ethics he brings to the practice of it.* 'Power does not change people [he once remarked]; it just shows them as they really are.' *We must hope Mujica stays clear of that group he has ridiculed: the ex-presidents who cannot refrain from telling their successors what to do!*

I conclude with three assessments from the final year of Mujica's presidency and a final paragraph that tries to draw together essential threads. The first opinion is that of journalist Roberto Elissalde (26 February 2015): 'Mujica presented himself as a representative of the bloke on the street and ended up being a point of reference for a particular way of being Uruguayan . . . Perhaps what stands out in [Mujica's presidency] is that the voice most listened to was that of those who have no voice, who don't exist, who are scarcely seen as people at all. Mujica did not make any dramatic turn to the left, didn't make the socialist revolution and didn't even get the trains to run more often. But he incorporated new actors and new voices into the nation's life and, for at least as long the left is in power, those actors and voices are not going away.'

The second is by Alfredo García, friend and editor of the weekly *Voces*, from its 400th issue on 29 August 2013:

'I don't know whether Mujica's government will leave us any great works. Even if it does, they will be many fewer than both he himself and the many of us who supported him were hoping for. What I can visualise is that his government leaves a democratic stamp not yet perceivable. Never before was there such a republican presidency. Never before did a political leader ask so many questions of us. Never before was life itself so important to the man who governed us. Never before did a president speak so much of love. Years will pass and Uruguayans will remember this contradictory old man who got us to think. Years will pass and presidents will come and go, but we will never forget that once, someone just like us became president. No, it will not be easy to forget Pepe's government.'

The last is from historian Gerardo Caetano in 2014: '[Mujica's] government will not go down in history as a great government, among other reasons because his signature projects have not really settled in. There has been poor management. In certain fundamental areas, like education, housing, infrastructure, investment in science and technology, there are important deficits. However, in many ways, there is a Uruguay before Mujica and another Uruguay after Mujica. Great politicians go down in history for many reasons, and one of them is the citizenry they helped to create . . . He will be remembered as someone who, in some measure, through his deeds and the concordance between his way of thinking and his way of living, reaffirmed that old adage so dear to Uruguay's sense of its own identity: "here nobody is better than anyone else".'

A revolutionary who opted to fight on under capitalist democracy after the failure of his and his comrades' attempt to overthrow it; a socialist not against private property, only the ruthless accumulation of it at the expense of the people as a whole; a libertarian whose sense of liberty is primarily collective always provided it leaves enough space and time for individuals to freely pursue their own happiness and fulfilment; a politician who works for a State providing that State is run for the benefit of all and not just a privileged few; an indefatigable worker who believes the only work really worth doing is that which helps yourself, your loved ones and your neighbours; a materialist who understands the spiritual value of sharing what you most need and feel free enough to give away; an elected parliamentarian who has little faith in either liberal democracy or parliamentarianism; a member of lower and upper houses of parliament who refuses to wear a suit and tie; finally, an autodidact philosopher who takes his habitual imagery from the natural world but is convinced that, since all humanity's fundamental problems stem from the way we see ourselves and relate to others, any solutions to them are primarily political.

This list of surprising juxtapositions and apparent contradictions could be extended or altered, but one essential aspect of Mujica's public and private personas would be clear in any version of it: his utter indifference and lack of fear or apprehension at being different or eccentric. This is because, at least in part, Mujica's view of any worthwhile society is one in which, like him, everyone has the right and opportunity to be what they are and to evolve into being whatever they become. This sense of social inclusiveness has guided all his militancy, policy making and his ideological quarrels with allies and adversaries alike, and has also determined that the changes required to implement it are so great, and many of their consequences so momentous, that they have been rejected by stronger forces more conservative or less forward-looking than those he can marshal or control. No matter. For a few short years we who live in Uruguay could catch enough of a glimpse of what such a society and culture might be for those who enjoyed it that we could relate it back to what the Tupamaros fought and died for as well as forward to what an Alain Badiou could see today of a resurgent left in France and elsewhere.

I grew up in municipal housing in Southern England in the early 1950s, but thanks to grammar school and university education (and government grants to do both), both as student and teacher (now retired) who still never preferably wears more than tea-shirt, jeans and a jacket, I can now listen pleasurably to Mahler, Schoenberg and Shostakovitch as I write this in Montevideo sitting in what was once famously called 'a room of my own' at a desk surrounded by CDs and books in several languages. I too believe what I enjoyed should not be the privilege of a few but freely available on a merit basis to those who want and need it as I did. Because of this I have tried to write a book that shares José 'Pepe' Mujica with its readers, in the hope that one day, not likely to be soon, there will be enough interested and empowered enough to begin that 'swarm', not of drone-like worker bees, but of those who believe their own freedom to be best expressed by the way they freely work and live in ways that further the freedom of others not necessarily like themselves.

Glossary

The Glossary comprises an alphabetical listing of essential Uruguayan proper names and terms. Elements in **bold** within a description have a separate entry.

Artigas, José 'Pepe' Seen as the founder of the nation of Uruguay out of the independence of wars of the early nineteenth century, Artigas in fact did not look to make Uruguay an independent country but rather an autonomous part of a confederation that would have included what is now Argentina. Artigas died defeated in embittered exile in Paraguay. Quarrelling between Argentina and Brazil coupled with Great Britain's need for a deep water trading port not controlled by either largely determined the conversion of Uruguay into an independent state. The Artigas legacy remains an ideological no-man's-land still fought over by all the main political parties in Uruguay.

Batlle, Jorge President from 2000 to 2005, Batlle presided over Uruguay's worst economic crisis since the 1930s in 2001–2. He handed the sash on to the **Broad Front**'s **Tabaré Vázquez** on 1 March 2005.

Batlle Berres, Luis Nephew of **José Batlle y Ordoñez**. President 1947–1951 and 1955–8. His second presidency marks the beginning of the long political and economic crisis that would result in the military coup in June 1973. His import substitution industry policies aided living standards of working classes.

Batlle y Ordoñez, José 'Pepe' Arguably the most famous man in Uruguayan twentieth century history. Put an end to civil war in 1904 and was President twice (1903–7 and 1911–1916). Founded a progressive liberal social welfare state (although full electoral democracy came later) whose culture and style bear his name: "Batllismo", still a yardstick for measuring social reform in Uruguay and still a sector in the **Colorado Party**.

Benedetti, Mario Until his death in 2009 at the age of eighty-nine, Benedetti was one of Uruguay's most widely read left-wing writers and journalists. Like Mujica, Benedetti was a lowly ranked candidate for the failed **Unión Popular** in 1962, an event that led him to recommend the left seek alternatives to electoral democracy. A sympathiser of the **MLN**, in 1971 he co-founded and co-led the '26 of March Movement', effectively a legal shop front for **MLN** supporters. In the same year, he dedicated his novel-in-verse *Juan Ángel's Birthday* to **MLN** founder **Raúl Sendic**.

Berreta, Tomás   Elected president in 1946. His sudden death in August 1947 brought vice-president **Batlle Berres** into power.

Blanco   The first and most combative name for the National Party, one of the two Uruguayan traditional political parties dating from the wars of independence against the Spanish empire and named after the colour (white) that distinguished them from the **Colorados**, their political adversaries from the same period. The National Party did not govern Uruguay till 1958, hence the insurrectionist tone of its original name, as, often fighting from the interior, they tried to assert the rights of small farmers and the rural population at large against their generally urban rulers, who usually also included the large rural estate holders.

Broad Front   Centre-left coalition founded in 1971 that allowed Socialists and Communists to combine forces for the first time and collaborate with other progressives from all parts of the political spectrum. The Front tripled the combined left vote in the 1971 elections to reach a promising 18% nationally. Its leaders and members were targeted by the repression of the late 1960s and early 1970s, and the whole Party was outlawed during the military dictatorship (1973–1985). Since re-democratisation, the Front has gone from success to success, first in opposition and then governing Montevideo since 1989 and the nation since 2005.

Castro, Fidel   Emblematic leader of the Cuban revolution that came to power in January 1959. Because the Cuban revolution has produced a one-party Communist state, Fidel (in Cuba it is considered unfriendly to refer to him as Castro) is regularly but erroneously labelled a 'dictator' in the right-wing or liberal democratic press. The influence of the Cuban example on the left everywhere in Latin America was immeasurable.

Colonización (Ley de)   A 1948 law that was intended to aid the State purchase of farming land to avoid its unproductive accumulation by large landowners interested only in returns on rising land prices. The latter prevented its adequate resourcing for many decades and, although recently reinforced and still in use, its results remain a matter of debate.

Colorado Party For two reasons, the more important of the two traditional Uruguayan political parties dating from independence days in the early nineteenth century. Firstly, it governed the country uninterruptedly for ninety-three years until the National Party's victory in 1958 (see **Blanco** entry), not good training for a party that has known opposition frequently since then. Secondly, it was the home of **José Batlle y Ordoñez**, and its fortunes have waxed and waned in part depending on the strength of the "Batllista" sector within it. The Colorado Party was controversially involved in both the imposition of the military dictatorship in 1973 and in the transition out of it in 1984–5.

Cordano, Lucy Much loved and admired mother of Mujica. He started working with her growing and selling flowers when a six-year-old after his father's untimely death. It was with her family's properties near Carmelo, close to the Argentine border, that Mujica first experienced cooperation among small farmers. Lucy should not be confused with **Lucía Topolansky**, Mujica's long-time partner and wife. Mujica's mother always used the English form of the name.

Erro, Enrique Radical Minister for Industry and Labour under National Party administration of 1958 (see **Blanco** entry). Mentor to Mujica in parliamentary politics and sympathiser with aims of guerrilla fighters. Ousted by his conservative National Party colleagues, he joined renegade Socialists and others to form the ill-fated **Unión Popular**, one of two left coalitions created to participate in the 1962 national elections.

Fernández Huidobro, Eleuterio Comrade and friend of Mujica in the **MLN**, and one of its founders and now its all but official historian, Fernández Huidobro was, like Mujica, one of the dictatorship's nine 'hostages'. He became a controversial Minister of Defence under President Mujica but was retained in the role by the second **Vázquez** administration.

FIDEL The acronym (after Cuban revolution leader **Fidel Castro**) for a coalition of groups and independents led by the Communist Party formed to fight the 1962 national elections. It fared better than the Socialist Party's rival grouping, the **Unión Popular**.

Frente Amplio See **Broad Front**.

Frugoni, Emilio Legendary leader of Socialist Party founded in 1910. His leadership was questioned after the success of the Cuban Revolution in 1959 suggested a new direction for the left, leading to a total split of his party in 1962, with disastrous electoral results (see also **Unión Popular**).

Gelman, Juan Argentine poet and guerrilla fighter. Friend and comrade of **Mario Benedetti,** Gelman is widely known in Uruguay through his long and eventually successful search there for his granddaughter, born while her parents were in prison after being 'disappeared' (and presumably killed) by the Argentine military. She was finally traced to 'adoptive parents' in Uruguay not long before Gelman himself died while a revered grandfather and much admired poet. The highly publicised case helped keep the whole issue of the 'disappeared' before the Uruguayan public eye. The granddaughter is now a deputy in the Uruguayan parliament.

Guevara, Ernesto 'Che' Legendary Argentine revolutionary doctor of medicine who fought alongside **Fidel Castro** in Cuba. Made a Cuban citizen, he served several important functions in the revolutionary government, making a tumultuous official visit to Uruguay in 1961. Frustrated behind a desk, he was eventually wounded, captured, tortured and executed in October 1967 while trying to put into practice his own call for 'many Vietnams' in the inhospitable jungles of Bolivia. Still a beacon in many revolutionary circles, 'Che' remains elsewhere an icon of 1960s youthful revolt.

Herrera, Luis Alberto de Historian and long-time National Party leader who died very shortly after its election victory in 1958 (see **Blanco** entry). Socially and politically conservative, he was nonetheless a virulent anti-imperialist, especially where the United States was concerned. His **Blanco** interpretation of Uruguay's history was important in Mujica's intellectual and political development.

Lacalle, Luis Alberto National Party president (1990–1995) and Mujica's chief rival in the 2009 elections. Despite class and political differences, Lacalle and Mujica remain on good personal terms, having met when both were politically committed adolescents.

MERCOSUR Abbreviated name of South America's much less productive version of the European Common Market. Founded with much fanfare in 1991, and based in Montevideo but frequently dominated by the local concerns of particular Argentine and Brazilian governments, MERCOSUR negotiations are difficult and have not led to much in the way of unity. Paraguay's long held refusal to allow the consensus required to accept Venezuela's request for entry is exemplary of the frustration felt by almost all participant countries, especially Uruguay, the prosperity, even survival, of whose tiny economy needs open international markets, especially in the region.

Methol Ferré, Alberto   Political historian and Catholic theologian, and author of the perpetually relevant 1967 classic *Uruguay as Problem* [*El Uruguay como problema*], reissued in 2015 with timely new commentary. Believed Uruguay was not viable as a separate country unless supported by regional unity as an alternative to overseas imperial interests. Prominent advocator of what became **MERCOSUR**, Methol Ferré died before its frustrations and limitations became too visible.

MLN   Spanish acronym for the Movement of National Liberation–**Tupamaros**, the most important urban guerrilla group in Uruguay and one of the best known throughout the world. Formed in the early 1960s, the MLN reached public attention in 1965 but became genuinely popular later in the decade as its 'armed propaganda' spread the truth about the levels of corruption in political and business circles. Forced into an all-out war with US-aided security forces, the MLN was all but entirely defeated by September 1972, ten months before the military coup that used it as excuse and justification. Involved with the MLN from its beginnings, Mujica became one of its leaders only in 1967. Imprisoned and tortured like many MLN members and other leftist and trade union activists, Mujica was one of the nine MLN 'hostages' held by the military as political blackmail pawns right through the negotiated transition back to civilian rule in 1985. They were eventually released in March that year.

MPP   Acronym for the Movement of Popular Participation. Formed in 1989, the MPP is in effect the post-dictatorship political expression of the **MLN** in legalised form as a major sector within the **Broad Front**. However, many original **MLN** members have rejected this watered down version of what they fought (and died) for. Mujica and his partner **Lucía Topolansky**, both senators, are still the MPP's leading spokespersons, though not for much longer if Mujica's promises of retirement are honoured.

Nardone, Benito   Kind of Uruguayan rural union leader whose proselytising over the radio in the 1950s was instrumental in getting the interior to vote for the National Party in the 1958 elections (see **Blanco** entry). He was rewarded with a government post but became a rabidly anti-communist, pro-McCarthy Cold War rabble-rouser. He was important in showing Uruguayan politicians (and Mujica) how to turn the radio into a propaganda tool.

Pacheco Areco, Jorge Never popularly elected **Colorado** president who took over power on the incumbent's death in December 1967. Governing by almost uninterrupted periods of state emergency laws, he bypassed a frequently hostile parliament and mounted an all-out war of repression supposedly against the **MLN** but actually against all those who supported or worked for left-wing or trade union organisations. He was succeeded in the 1971 elections by another right-wing **Colorado** president, Juan María Bordaberry, who became the civilian front for the military takeover in June 1973.

Pérez, Amodio By the early 1970s, he had a place on the **MLN** executive close to Mujica and the other leaders. Captured (or made to appear so), he is accused by all his former comrades of having betrayed what remained of the organisation to the military and security police. Pérez in turn accuses them of using him as scapegoat for the **MLN**'s own failures and trying to kill or frame him in revenge for his public disclosure of their faults and errors. What he has never explained is why the military arranged for him and his then partner, **Alicia Rey**, to have new lives in Spain under false names while the rest of the **MLN** were incarcerated and tortured in Uruguayan jails. Pérez returned to Uruguay in 2015 to promote his own published version of **MLN** history, only to be met by numerous legal complications that have him currently under house arrest.

PISA Acronym for Program of International Student Assessment. Uruguayan students have been doing far worse on this annual testing of educational abilities of fifteen-year-olds than just about all their Latin American counterparts. While teachers and their union representatives make cases for the special situation of Uruguayan schools and students, opposition spokespeople see it as clear evidence that there has been an embarrassingly steady decline in Uruguayan public education standards under the **Broad Front** governments, despite genuinely large expenditure increases. Debate rages on, but that the public education system, especially at secondary level, needs real reform is agreed by all. There is just no consensus on how to do it.

Real de Azúa, Carlos One of Uruguay's most influential political and cultural historians of the mid twentieth century, Real de Azúa started out as a right-wing Uruguayan Catholic supporter of Spanish dictator General Francisco Franco and ended up a **MLN** sympathiser and supporter of the **Broad Front**. His re-readings of history written with densely baroque rhetorical flare have stirred the minds of three generations.

Rey, Alicia   Close associate and partner of **Amodio Pérez** and an active member of the **MLN**, she was aided by the military to escape with him to Spain under false names so they could start new lives there. Unlike him, however, Alicia Rey has never come out of hiding or disguise to explain herself or help her former friend and comrade in his quest to re-establish his reputation in Uruguay.

Sanguinetti, Julio María   Twice president of Uruguay (1985–1990 and 1995–2000), Sanguinetti was also a minister in the government that led to the coup. He has become the **Colorado** historian of the whole period, justifying his party's and the right's approach to the threat from the left during the whole period from the 1960s up to his own presidencies.

Saravia, Aparicio   Last armed **Blanco** insurrectionist from the interior. Lost out to **Batlle y Ordóñez** in 1904. Fought for the labourers and small farmers so dear to Mujica, who had a photograph of Saravia at his bedside during childhood and adolescence.

Sendic, Raúl   Renegade socialist and **Blanco** lawyer dedicated to aiding the poverty-stricken and exploited cane and rice workers of Uruguay's subtropical North in the 1950s, Sendic became the leading intellectual and political light behind the **MLN**, of which he was both the founder and its first clandestine warrior. Persecuted and almost martyred by the Uruguayan military, he survived to persuade the incarcerated **MLN** leadership that unarmed, legal political militancy was the best way forward for them after the dictatorship. Dying in 1989, he lived just long enough to see the successful beginnings of such work.

Terra, Gabriel   President famous for organising a peaceful coup against himself in 1933 so he could govern by decree during the 1930s depression. Democracy returned in 1942 as the Second World War brought prosperity to a formally neutral Uruguay and the Allies successes on the battlefield and in the air eroded the position of the Uruguayan Axis supporters, of whom the **Colorado** Terra was one.

Topolansky, Lucía   Mujica's long-time partner and his wife from 2005. Met when both were active members of the **MLN** in the 1960s. Like Mujica, Topolansky was imprisoned throughout the dictatorship, but did not have to undergo the same degree of ill treatment. Like Mujica, she remains an active senator and is second to him in the leadership of the **MPP**, their **Broad Front** sector.

Tupamaros   The **MLN**'s own alternative name for themselves. Not so much based, as widely believed, on Tupac Amaru, the legendary Inca rebel against Spanish invasion and plunder in Peru, but on the name given to impoverished peasants in a novel, *Ismael*, by Uruguayan author Eduardo Acevedo Díaz. The relevance is completed by the fact that in 1935 the Communist author took up arms in an ill-fated **Aparicio Saravia**-like revolt by peasants from the interior against their Montevideo rulers and employers.

UNASUR   Continental political counterpart to **MERCOSUR** that seeks to promote cooperation among South American countries. Frequently the despair of those who believe in it and only too easily the butt of gleeful satire of those who do not.

Unión Popular [UP]   Grouped around renegades from the Socialist Party but led by **Enrique Erro**, the UP was one of two left-wing coalitions (the other being **FIDEL**) formed to fight the 1962 national elections. Because it split the Socialist Party and due to last minute defections, the UP's poor vote left the Socialists with no parliamentary representation for the first time in the party's fifty-odd year history. Both Mujica and the writer **Mario Benedetti** stood as low-listed candidates for the UP. Its failure marked both their lives.

Vázquez, Tabaré   Leader of the **Broad Front** since the early 1990s (except for the period of Mujica's presidency) and twice president of the nation (2005–2010 and 2015–2020), Vázquez is a working class boy made good. Originally of Socialist Party background but now a **Broad Front** Independent and a wealthy cancer specialist with a large stake in one of Uruguay's richest health care providers, Vázquez marks the middle-class, moderate face of the **Broad Front**, whose non-presumptuous, working-class side is exemplified by Mujica. The debates between the two approaches and the nuances to them provided by its different sectors are what makes the **Front** genuinely **Broad**, and often means that the most creative opposition to which ever side is uppermost comes from within.

Walsh, Rodolfo   Argentine revolutionary, writer and translator. 'Disappeared' by the military after the 1976 coup in Argentina. Whereabouts still unknown.

Chronology

The Chronology provides a brief timeline of major events in Mujica's life and Uruguayan context.

1935   *20 May*: Mujica born in Paso de la Arena, then a semi-rural suburb of Montevideo.

1944   Father Demetrio Mujica dies.

1947   March. Begins high school and political miliatcny with anarchisr student group.

1948   Begins to take cycling seriously, reaching national qualification standard over the next few years, but takes it no further. Cycle rides bring him his first contact with the rural interior.

1951   Begins but does not finish law preparatory course. Audits classes in the Humanities Faculty at the University, where he benefits from literature and composition classes taught by Spanish Republican exile José Bergamín and Uruguayan novelist Francisco 'Paco' Espínola, as well as open courses in Uruguayan history.

1954   Votes for the first time and helps Socialist Party.

1956   Meets Enrique Erro and joins his youth sector in the National Party.

1958–60 Part of Erro's team during his conflictive stint as Minister of Labour and Industry.

1959   January. Fidel Castro's triumphant revolutionary army enters Havana, Cuba.

1960   Pro-worker Erro forced to resign from Ministry.

1960–1 Mujica visits Soviet Union, China and Cuba as official delegate of Erro's Youth Movement.

1962   Mujica joins Erro as part of Unión Popular [UP], socialist-led coalition group created as option in November national elections. Mujica himself a low-rung candidate in Montevideo. UP's failure convinces Mujica that the left must find a new way of doing politics.

1963   First action by what would become the MLN (stole

weapons from shooting club). Mujica involved with groups talking about armed revolution.

1964 Mujica imprisoned for first time (eight-month sentence). Pretended to be ordinary criminal though caught stealing resources to help rice and cane workers led by Raúl Sendic, founder of the MLN. The word 'Tupamaros' first used publicly in propaganda painted on Montevideo walls.

1965 First official Tupamaros document linking struggle for national liberation with liberation of whole continent from foreign imperialist interests.

1967 Mujica does both clandestine MLN work and legal normal life.

1968 Mujica's first armed action for MLN. Bomb destroyed transmission tower of radio station run by Colorado Party. Also a participant in MLN's first political kidnapping.

1969 Finally forced permanently underground by discovery of weapons he had left with a friend. 8 October: to mark first anniversary of 'Che' guevara's assassination in Bolivia, Mujica participates in the taking of the rural town of Pando by MLN forces. Only time in his life he wears a suit and tie; he was dressed as a mourning relative in a funeral procession.

1970 Seriously wounded in a bar after being recognised and betrayed by off-duty policeman (later killed by MLN). After two months in military hospital, Mujica is transferred to a prison in the Montevideo seaside suburb of Punta Carretas (the prison is now part of a large shopping mall next to the Sheraton Hotel).

1971 *6 September.* Part of escape with 110 other political and common prisoners organised by the MLN (and perhaps permitted by the police for tactical reasons). This mass breakout made the Guinness Book of Records.
October. Mujica back in jail after being betrayed by one of the common criminals who had accompanied him in the Punta Carretas escape.
November. Broad Front's first national election appearance. Achieves 18% of the national vote, but came second in Montevideo. The Front received critical support from the MLN, which declared a unilateral truce for the

campaign period. This gesture was not reciprocated by the security forces which, with paramilitary aid, did as much as possible to make the Front's perfectly legal existence and electoral participation as difficult and dangerous as they could.

1972   *April.* Mujica again escapes from Punta Carretas. MLN begins a kind of tit-for-tat targeted execution war with the ever-better prepared security forces.

May. Mujica escapes from blown MLN hideout through the Montevideo sewer network. Involved in several shootouts with police.

June. Mujica and Lucía Topolansky given shelter by Enrique Erro and his wife.

July. First major betrayals by captured MLN members. The net is finally closing in.

August. Mujica taken prisoner for the fourth and last time. He will not escape again.

1973   *February.* Military communiqués hint at their political intentions while holding out apparent olive branches to left.

April. Parliament debates the Executive's request to lift Enrique Erro's politician's immunity which would make him liable to arrest for his contacts with the MLN. Parliament rejects the possibility.

26 June. The military dissolve parliament and the civic-military dictatorship begins.

September. Mujica, along with other imprisoned MLN leaders, start their long period of isolation, torture and subhuman confinement conditions (often literally in holes dug in the ground). Mujica was not alone in being driven to near insanity during this period. In 1983–4, the military accepted their time was up and all their prisoners would have to be released in acceptable shape. Part of the ensuing negotiations was a gradual relaxing of prison conditions for political detainees, including even the MLN 'hostages'.

1985   *March.* First post-authoritarian civil government under Clorado president Julio María Sanguinetti. Mujica and the other 'hostages' finally released under general amnesty. MLN quickly begins new phase as legal political organisation and Mujica gives first speech as chief spokesman for it. MLN leaders travel the country having informal meetings and conversations with all and sundry to investigate the state of post-dictatorship Uruguay and to show themselves to their potential electorate.

1986   MLN requests formal admission to join Broad Front centre-left coalition, a proposal that causes rifts in both organisations. First signs of what will be a long debate within the MLN between the so-called proletarians, who want it to be a political and military organisation ready to take up arms again if needs be, and those like Mujica who, following resolutions taken by the leadership while still in jail, are wholly committed to turning the electorate leftwards but within the rules of the Uruguayan constitution.

Military granted impunity by parliament for crimes against humanity committed during the dictatorship.

1989   Broad Front wins control of Montevideo's Town Hall under Tabaré Vázquez as Mayor, a position it still holds though with constitutionally required changes of personnel. First attempt to repeal military 'impunity' law by referendum fails.

MLN finally admitted into Broad Front, where they create the Movement for Popular Participation [MPP]. Led by Mujica, the MPP is the formal political and electoral expression of the MLN, but includes other smaller groups that seek association with it.

1994   Vázquez and the Broad Front lose national elections in part because of violent street actions led by the so-called proletarians within the MLN in favour of Basque nationalist militants due to be extradited to Spain. As a result, the vast majority of MLN members finally accept there can be no popular support for non-electoral options in post-dictatorship Uruguay, siding with the MPP and Vázquez. Mujica is elected as deputy in the lower house.

1996   Colorado and National parties join to win popular approval for constitutional change requiring second round ballottage between presidential candidates if the majority party has not gained more than fifty percent of the vote in the first round that decides parliamentary representation.

1999   Vázquez and Broad Front lose national elections only because of combined Colorado and National vote in second round. Mujica elected senator for the MPP.

2004   *31 October.* Vázquez and Broad Front win national elections in the first round, with a majority in both houses.

2005   Mujica appointed Minister for Agriculture and Lucía Topolansky enters parliament as MPP senator. She and Mujica marry.

2008   Mujica resigns his Ministry to campaign for selection as Broad Front presidential candidate in 2009. After much internal wrangling, he wins Broad Front approval against Minister of Finance Danilo Astori, the candidate recommended by President Vázquez as his successor. Astori eventually runs as Mujica's Vice-President.

2009   *November.* Mujica elected President in second round run-off against the National Party's Luis Alberto Lacalle. Second referendum to repeal military's 'impunity' for crimes during dictatorship lost, though more narrowly than the first back in 1989.

2010   *March.* Mujica takes office and controversially refuses to live in the official presidential residence, preferring life with his spouse on their modest small holding in Rincón del Cerro, an outlying district of Montevideo only a bus ride from where he was born seventy-five years earlier.

2012   In a Rio de Janeiro environment summit, Mujica makes the first of a series of anti-imperialist, anti-capitalist and pro-socialist speeches delivered over the next few years in ever more important public forums that bring him very favourable international attention not uniformly matched in his home country.

2013   Attempts to address international judicial criticism of Uruguay's 'impunity' law via formal repeal by act of parliament declared unconstitutional by the nation's supreme court.

2012–14   Mujica government legalises same-sex marriage, abortion and personal use and cultivation of marihuana, sale of which will be supervised and taxed by the state as part of a campaign against drug trafficking and its accompanying crime. This latter provision is being implemented very slowly by the current government.

2015   March. Mujica returns to being plain 'senator' after handing the presidential sash to Tabaré Vázquez to begin his second presidency and the Broad Front's third successive national administration.

May. Mujica supports his wife's losing run at being Mayor of Montevideo.

November. Mujica and Lucía Topolansky announce their intention to stand down as senators and MPP leaders in April 2016. Ongoing bickering over executive policy and decisions within the Broad Front seem to indicate, in part at least, the notable absence of the strong people's republic tone Mujica brought to government ranks in his five years as president.

Sources

The following list includes only materials used in the course of writing this book. It is divided into four sections: Mujica, MLN–Tupamaros, Works of General Reference and Periodicals. Full details of books and occasional scholarly articles are given but the Periodicals have been limited to a list of titles, mostly of daily or weekly publications from Montevideo, of which repeated use has been made in either their print or digital versions.

Mujica

Arbilla, Danilo (ed.): *Mujica en* Búsqueda: *trece años en 21 reportajes* (Montevideo, Búsqueda/Fin de Siglo, 2009).

Blixen, Samuel: *El sueño del Pepe* (Montevideo, Trilce, 2009).

Campodónico, Miguel Ángel: *Mujica* [1999] (23rd ed., Montevideo, Fin de Siglo, 2014).

Caula, Nelson & Silva, Alberto: *Ana la guerrillera. Una historia de Lucía Topolansky* (Montevideo, Ediciones B, 2011).

Danza, Andrés & Tulbovitz, Ernesto: *Una oveja negra al poder. Confesiones e intimidades de Pepe Mujica* (Montevideo, Sudamericana, 2015).

Domínguez, María Noel: *José Mujica: la realidad, la angustia, la esperanza* (Montevideo, Ediciones de la Banda Oriental, 2005).

Fernández, Nelson: *Quién es quién en el gobierno de Mujica* (Montevideo, Fin de Siglo, 2010).

García, Alfredo: *Pepe: coloquios* (Montevideo, Fin de Siglo, 2009).

Gilio, María Esther: *Pepe Mujica: De tupamaro a Presidente* (Buenos Aires, Capital Intelectual, 2010).

Instituto de Ciencia Política: *Política en tiempos de Mujica I– III* (3 Vols., Montevideo, Estuario, 2011, 2012, 2013).

Israel, Sergio: *Mujica, el florista presidente* (Montevideo, Fin de Siglo, 2010).

——: *Pepe Mujica el presidente. Una investigación no autorizada* (Montevideo, Planeta, 2014).

Lucas, Kintto: *Tal cual es . . . El camino de José Mujica a la Presidencia* (Quito, Tintají, 2012).

Mazzeo, Mario: *Charlando con Pepe Mujica* (Montevideo, Trilce, 2002).

—— (ed.): *José Pepe Mujica/Rodrigo Arocena: cuando la izquierda gobierne* (Montevideo, Trilce, 2003).

Percy, Allan: *Mujica. Una biografía inspirada* (Montevideo, Ediciones B, 2015).

Pernas, Walter: *Comandante Facundo. El revolucionario Pepe Mujica* (Montevideo, Aguilar, 2013).

Rabuffetti, Mauricio: *José Mujica, la revolución tranquila* (Montevideo, Aguilar, 2014).

Tucci, Mariano: *Historias blancas de un hombre de izquierda* (Montevideo, Planeta, 2014).

MLN–Tupamaros

Aldrighi, Clara: *La izquierda armada. Ideología, ética e identidad en el MLN–Tupamaros* (Montevideo, Trilce, 2001).

——: *Memorias de insurgencia. Historias de vida y militancia en el MLN–Tupamaros 1965–1975* (Montevideo, Ediciones d ela Banda Oriental, 2009).

Archivochile.com: Originals of documents by and about MLN in Spanish. Free and indispensable.

Brum, Pablo: *The Robin Hood Guerrillas: The Epic Journey of Uruguay's Tupamaros* (Author's ebook, Amazon, 2014).

Churchill, Lindsey: *Becoming the Tupamaros: Solidarity and Transnational Revolutionaries in Uruguay and the United States* (Nashville, Vanderbilt University Press, 2014).

Fernández Huidobro, Eleuterio: *Historia de los Tupamaros* [1986–7] (Montevideo, Ediciones de la Banda Oriental, 2012).

Garcé, Adolfo: *Donde hubo fuego. El proceso de adaptación del MLN–Tupamaros a la legalidad y a la competencia electoral (1985–2004)* (4th ed., Montevideo, Fin de Siglo, 2009).

Gatto, Hebert: *El cielo por asalto. El Movimiento de Liberación Nacional (Tupamaros) y la izquierda uruguaya (1963–1972)* (Montevideo, Taurus, 2004).

Gilio, María Esther: *La guerrilla tupamara* (Montevideo, Marcha, 1971).

Guerrero Palermo, Gustavo: *Los orígenes del MLN en el interior. El rol de Sendic* (Montevideo, Fin de Siglo, 2014).

Gutiérrez, Ángel: *Los tupamaros en la década de los sesenta* (Mexico, Extemporáneos, 1978).

Labrousse, Alain: *Los tupamaros* (trans. Rodolfo Walsh, Buenos Aires, Editorial Tiempo Contemporáneo, 1971).
——: *The Tupamaros* (trans. Dinah Livingstone, London, Penguin, 1973).
——: *Una historia de los Tupamaros* (trans. Laura Graciela Klang, Montevideo, Fin de Siglo, 2009).
Lessa, Alfonso: *La revolución imposible. Los tupamaros y el fracaso de la vía armada en el Uruguay del siglo XX* [2010] (Montevideo, Debolsillo, 2013).
Mazzeo, Mario: *El MPP: orígenes, ideas, protagonistas* (Montevideo, Trilce, 2005).
MLN: *Actas tupamaras* (Buenos Aires, Schapire, 1971).
Rey Tristán, Eduardo: *A la vuelta de la esquina. La izquierda revolucionaria uruguaya 1955–1973* (Montevideo, Fin de Siglo, 2006).
Sasso, Rolando: *Tupamaros: Los comienzos* (Montevideo, Fin de Siglo, 2010).
——: *Tupamaros. El auge de la propaganda armada* (Montevideo, Fin de Siglo, 2012).
——: *Tupamaros. La derrota* (Montevideo, Fin de Siglo, 2015).
Tagliferro, Gerardo: *Adiós Robin Hood. 7 tupamaros, 40 años después* (Montevideo, Fin de Siglo, 2008).

Works of General Reference
Anderson, Benedict: *Imagined Communities* (revised edition, London, Verso, 2006).
Badiou, Alain: *D'un désastre obscur. Droit, État, Politique* [1991] (Paris, L'aube, 2012).
——: *De un desastre obscuro. Sobre el fin de la verdad del Estado* (Buenos Aires, Amorrortu, 2007).
——: 'Of an Obscure Disaster: On the End of the Truth of State', *lacanian ink*, 22 (2003), pp. 58–89. [This translation is abridged and often confusing, hence the need for the previous entries].
——: *Ethics: An Essay on the Understanding of Evil* (London, Verso, 2012).
——: *Philosophy for Militants* (London, Verso, 2015).
——: *The Rebirth of History* (London, Verso, 2012).
Bosteels, Bruno: *The Actuality of Communism* (London, Verso, 2011).
——: *Marx and Freud in Latin America* (London, Verso, 2012).
Broquetas, Magdalena: *La trama autoritaria. Derechas y violencia en*

Uruguay (1958–1966) (Montevideo, Ediciones de la Banda Oriental, 2014).

Debray, Régis: 'Socialism: A Life-Cycle', *New Left Review*, 46 (2007), pp. 5–28.

Derrida, Jacques: *The Politics of Friendship* [1994] (London, Verso, 2005).

——: *Specters of Marx* [1993] (New York, Routledge, 2006).

Gregory, Stephen: *Intellectuals and Left Politics in Uruguay, 1958–2006* (Eastbourne, Sussex Academic Press, 2009).

——: *El rostro tras la página. Mario Benedetti y el fracaso de una política del prójimo* (Montevideo, Estuario, 2014).

Lessa, Francesca: *¿Justicia o impunidad? Cuentas pendientes en el Uruguay post-dictadura* (Montevideo, Debate, 2014) [translation of unseen English original: *Memory and Transitional Justice in Argentina and Uruguay: Against Impunity* (Palgrave MacMillan, 2013)].

Marchesi, Aldo (ed.): *Ley de caducidad, un tema inconcluso. Momentos, actores y argumentos (1986–2013)* (Montevideo, Trilce, 2013).

Méndez Vives, Enrique: *500 años. Lo esencial de la historia uruguaya* (Montevideo, Ediciones de la Banda Oriental, 2014).

Methol Ferré, Alberto: *El Uruguay como problema* [1967] (Montevideo, HUM, 2015).

Nahum, Benjamín (ed.): *1960–2010 Medio siglo de historia uruguaya* (Montevideo, Ediciones de la Banda Oriental, 2012).

Panizza, Francisco: 'Late Institutionalisation and Early Modernisation: The Emergence of Uruguay's Liberal Democratic Political Order', *Journal of Latin American Studies*, 29 (1997), pp. 667–691.

Rico, Álvaro (ed.): *Cómo votaron los partidos en el plebiscito contra la caducidad en 2009 y la historia de la impunidad 2006–2013* (Montevideo, Trilce, 2014).

Ross, Kristin: *The Emergence of Social Space: Rimbaud and the Paris Commune* (London, Verso, 2008).

——: *Communal Luxury. The Political Luxury of the Paris Commune* (London, Verso, 2015).

Vierci, Pablo: *ellas 5* (Montevideo, Aguaclara, 2014).

Periodicals

El Observador.
El País.

Brecha.
Búsqueda.
Caras y Caretas.
Ladiaria.
La República.
LaRed21 (online only).
Lento.
Voces.

Index

Afro-Uruguayan, 103
Aldrighi, Clara, 24
Amir, Kimal, 24
Anarchism, 16, 63, 69
Anarchist, 16–17, 71, 74, 76, 109
Argentina, viii, 3, 5, 11, 17, 25, 30, 32, 41, 57, 66–67, 82–84, 98, 103–104, 132, 139
Argentine, 24, 42, 57, 85, 97–98, 103–104, 134–135, 139
Artigas, José, 51–52, 78, 132
Astori, Danilo, 97–98, 105, 144
Australia, 19, 26
Autonomy, 100–101, 120–121

Badiou, Alain, viii–x, xii, 54, 56, 63–64, 76, 79, 89, 117–118, 123, 125, 130
Ballottage, 57, 143
Batlle Berres, Luis, 10, 18–20, 132–133
Batlle y Ordoñez, José, 18, 69, 132, 134
Batlle, Jorge, 4–5, 10, 18–20, 52, 57, 69, 78, 81, 94, 132–134, 138
Batllista, 73, 134
Benedetti, Mario, vii–viii, xii, 28–29, 70, 132, 135, 139
Bergamín, José, 14–15, 110, 140
Berreta, Tomás, 10, 18, 133
Biology, 13–14, 34, 44, 55, 108
Blanco, 9, 20–21, 52, 133–136, 138
Boadas, Pedro, 17
Brazil, 25, 32, 35, 67, 83, 104, 118–119, 132
Brazilian, 104, 135

Broad Front, viii, 2–6, 20, 29, 39–40, 45, 47, 49, 51, 55, 57–59, 64, 66–67, 73–74, 77, 81–82, 84, 86–90, 93, 96–98, 102–103, 105, 108–109, 114, 125, 132–134, 136–139, 141, 143–145
Brum, Pablo, 24

Caetano, Gerardo, 1–2, 5, 129
Cane workers, 32–33, 141
Canessa, Marta, 4
Capitalism, x, 6, 16, 20–21, 35, 49–50, 58–59, 66, 68–72, 77, 79, 81, 83, 92–93, 95, 114, 116–117, 125
Capitalist, vii, 2, 26, 63, 66–67, 69, 75, 82–83, 99, 103, 114, 124, 129, 144
Castro, Fidel, 23, 121, 133–135, 140
Cerro, 27, 144
Cervantes, Miguel de, 14–15, 71
Chávez, Hugo, 104
China, 22, 25, 28, 67, 80, 83, 88, 104, 110, 140
Clandestine, 11, 28, 31, 35–36, 38, 54, 84, 127, 138, 141
Climate change, vi, 3, 26, 99
Colorado, 4, 9–10, 20, 36, 39, 57, 66, 81, 85, 87, 90, 97, 132, 134, 137–138, 141, 143–144
Communism, viii–x, 30, 63–64, 69, 76
Communist, viii, x, 14–17, 19, 22, 24, 28–29, 33–34, 45–46, 48, 54, 60, 69, 76, 88, 133–134, 136, 139

Communist Party, 16, 22, 28, 45, 60, 69, 88, 134
Community of Latin American and Caribbean Nations, 123, 125
Constitution, 4, 8, 18, 38, 40, 54, 75–76, 84, 104–105, 126, 143
Cooperation, 42, 59, 83, 99, 102–103, 134, 139
Cooperative, 2, 12, 15, 17, 19, 55, 70, 102
Cordano, Lucy (and family), 8–9, 12, 14–15, 21, 134
Cuba, viii, 22, 28, 41, 49, 80, 103–105, 119, 121–122, 133, 135, 140
Cultural change, 100, 122, 126
Culture, 4, 6, 10, 16, 18, 38, 43, 56, 61, 69–70, 72, 77, 93, 100, 106, 111–112, 118, 120, 124, 126, 130, 132

Darwin, Charles, 59
Delgado, María Auxiliadora, 5
Democracy, vii, x, xii, 2, 4, 8, 20, 23, 26, 39, 49–53, 59, 63, 67–69, 72, 74–77, 79, 81, 87, 89, 93, 113, 118, 121, 126–127, 129–130, 132–133, 138
Democratic, vii, ix–x, xii, 4–6, 18, 28–30, 49, 53, 58, 68, 71, 75, 79–81, 88, 90, 102, 105, 109, 129, 133
Derrida, Jacques, viii–x, 53, 63–64
Disappeared, 24, 42, 58, 84–85, 106, 135, 139

Ecology, 13
Economics, vii, x, 23, 33, 58, 63, 65, 82–83, 87, 124
Economy, 2, 18, 20, 23, 35, 57, 64, 66, 83, 88, 94, 97, 99, 110, 113, 120, 124, 136
Education, ix, 6, 13, 15–16, 38–39, 55, 83–84, 93, 98–102,

106–107, 112–113, 118, 122, 129–130, 137
Egalitarian, 34, 47, 69, 103
Elections, vii–viii, 8, 19–20, 22, 27–28, 38–39, 50, 57, 82, 87, 89–90, 113, 133–137, 139–140, 143–144
Electoral, vii, xii, 29, 49–50, 77, 87–88, 90, 105, 132–133, 135, 142–143
Elissalde, Roberto, 128
Elite, 6, 16, 23, 29, 36, 49, 98
Erro, Enrique, 19–23, 27–28, 36, 134, 139–140, 142
Espínola, Francisco 'Paco', 14–15, 140

Farm, 6, 10, 13, 18, 94–95, 103
Farmer, 111
Farming, 11, 14, 71, 93–96, 133
Fernández Huidobro, Eleuterio, 24, 44, 92, 134
FIDEL, 23, 28–29, 121, 133–135, 139–140
Finland, 94, 103
Flower, 7, 11
Frugoni, Emilio, 8, 19, 134

García Linera, Álvaro, ix
García, Alfredo, 129
Gatto, Hebert, 24
Gay marriage, 103
Gelman, Juan, 85, 135
Global, vi, ix, 50, 63, 68, 82, 93, 113, 120–121
Globalisation, 67, 93, 113, 120, 123
Guerrilla, vi, viii–ix, 3, 6–7, 11, 17, 19, 23–24, 27–28, 31, 34, 41, 46–49, 70, 79, 81, 83–85, 87, 109, 115, 124, 134–136
Guevara, Ernesto 'Che', 23, 30–31, 37, 49, 51, 61, 135, 141
Guillén, Abraham, 17

Herrera, Luis Alberto de, 21, 135
Hierarchical, 34, 61, 69, 120
Hierarchy, 73, 75
History, 5, 8, 13–16, 18, 20–21,
    23–26, 33, 43, 52–55, 59–60,
    63–65, 71, 82, 85–86, 90, 93,
    95, 99, 107, 109, 112,
    117–118, 120–127, 129, 132,
    135, 137–140
Horizontal, 12, 34, 69, 73
Hostages, 33, 41–42, 51, 80, 134,
    136, 142
Housing, 2, 92, 98, 102–103, 114,
    129–130
Humanities, 13, 65, 110, 140

Inequality, 65, 79, 125
Integration, 83, 103, 105
Intellectual, ix, 12, 14–16, 28,
    32–34, 44–45, 58, 79, 111–
    112, 116, 124, 135, 138

Labrousse, Alain, 24, 48
Lacalle Pou, Luis, 4, 58
Lacalle, Luis Alberto, 4, 22, 46,
    57–58, 70, 81, 135, 144
Landowner, 9, 19, 32
Left, vii–x, xii, 2, 5–6, 12, 14, 16,
    19–24, 27–29, 31–35, 37–40,
    46–48, 50, 52, 54–69, 71–73,
    76–77, 79–84, 86–90, 92–93,
    95, 99–101, 105, 108–109,
    111, 113, 115–117, 119, 121,
    123, 125–134, 137–143
Lenin, Vladimir, 60, 68, 80, 92,
    109, 116
Liberal, 18, 23, 26, 28–29, 50, 52,
    61, 63, 65, 69, 75, 77, 79,
    88–89, 93, 97, 105, 111, 130,
    132–133
Liberalism, 2, 5, 68–69
Libertarian, 3, 16, 22, 27, 34, 54–
    55, 61, 68–69, 75, 80, 89, 97,
    119, 129
Libertarianism, 69
Lilies, 10

Maduro, Nicolás, 104–105
Marihuana, 103, 144
Marx, Karl, viii–ix, 45, 53, 63–64,
    68, 80
Marxist, 16, 45–46, 54, 69, 89,
    118
MERCOSUR, 26, 67, 83, 98,
    104, 135–136, 139
Methol Ferré, Alberto, 26, 83, 136
Militancy, viii–ix, 4, 27, 47, 54,
    83, 86, 130, 138
Militant, viii, x, 7, 11, 17, 24, 27,
    33, 45, 49, 55–56, 62–63,
    80–81, 86, 91, 93, 99, 108–
    109, 118, 127
MLN (Movement of National
    Liberation), 23–29, 31–33,
    35–43, 45, 47–54, 57, 60,
    79–81, 83, 86–92, 105, 109,
    115, 121–122, 124, 127, 133–
    134, 136–143
MLN documents, 49
MPP (Movement for Popular
    Participation), 87–90, 97,
    108–109, 136, 139, 143–145

Nardone, Benito, 22, 136
Nation, viii, 2, 21, 25–26, 43, 47,
    52, 54–55, 57, 68, 71, 76, 78,
    81–83, 85, 90, 92, 97, 99–100,
    103–104, 110, 126, 128,
    132–133, 139, 144
National Party, 4, 20–22, 27, 30,
    57, 66, 81, 97, 133–136, 140,
    144
Neo-liberalism, 5
New Zealand, 19, 68, 94
Nordic countries, 102
Norway, 68, 114
Nostalgia, 55, 128

Organisation of American States,
    20, 30

Pacheco Areco, Jorge, 38, 137
Palme, Olof, 68, 116

Pando, 37, 141
Panza, Sancho, 1–4, 52, 71
Paraguay, 104, 132, 135
Parliament, vii, ix, 8, 18, 27, 38,
    46, 54, 57, 74–77, 80, 82, 85,
    90–93, 99, 104–105, 108, 110,
    113, 130, 135, 137, 142–144
Parliamentarianism, 63, 76, 81,
    130
Parliamentary, 47, 74–77, 91, 105,
    134, 139, 143
Participation, 28, 42, 50, 60, 70–
    74, 77, 79, 87–88, 90, 92,
    102, 121, 136, 142–143
Paso de la Arena, 9, 14, 140
Peasant Support Movement, 32
Pérez, Amodio, 41, 137–138
Philosopher, viii, 2, 44–78, 89,
    110, 130
Philosophy, viii–ix, xii, 2–3, 13,
    16, 53, 55–56, 58, 69, 80,
    110, 118, 123–124
PISA, 107, 137
Plan Juntos, 102, 114
Politics, vii–ix, xii, 2, 4, 13, 15–17,
    26, 44–46, 50, 54–56, 58–59,
    63–64, 72, 77, 79–80, 82, 88–
    89, 93, 110, 113, 115,
    120–125, 127–128, 134, 140
Pot, Pol, 10, 62
Pou, Julia, 4, 58
Poverty, 9, 11, 51, 65, 68–69, 84,
    98, 101–102, 107, 124–125,
    138
Public education, 84, 98, 106, 137

Quixote, Don, 1–2, 4, 15, 52, 71

Real de Azúa, Carlos, 31, 137
Redistribution, 64, 69, 72, 84,
    107–108
Republic, 14, 24–25, 29, 31, 51,
    70, 75, 145
Republican, 10, 31, 58, 75, 102,
    115, 126–127, 129, 140
Republicanism, 103

Revolution, vii, xii, 23, 30–31, 35,
    37, 44, 47–50, 52–53, 59–60,
    63, 66, 71–72, 75, 77, 89, 92,
    104, 122–123, 128, 133–134,
    141
Revolutionary, 22–26, 30, 32,
    46–48, 50, 52, 58, 71, 74–75,
    80, 88–89, 104–105, 114,
    120–122, 129, 135, 139–140
Rey Tristán, Eduardo, 23–24
Rey, Alicia, 23–24, 41, 137–138
Rice workers, 32, 138
Right, 15, 22, 27, 29–31, 33, 35,
    41, 46–47, 53–54, 59, 65, 71,
    83–85, 97–99, 101, 104–107,
    109, 111, 114, 117, 119, 122,
    128, 130, 133, 136–138
Rincón del Cerro, 144
Rio + 20, 113

Sanguinetti, Julio María, 4, 81–82,
    85, 97, 138, 142
Santiago de Cuba, 121
Scandinavian, 13
Self-help, 2, 12, 84, 103, 114
Sendic, Raúl, 32–33, 35–36,
    39–40, 45, 48, 50–51, 53,
    79–80, 86–87, 90, 117, 133,
    138, 141
Socialism, vii, x, 2, 16, 23, 34–35,
    50, 52, 59–62, 64, 68–70, 77,
    80, 105, 114–116, 118
Socialist, vii, x, xii, 8, 14, 17, 19,
    22, 26–29, 31–33, 35, 49, 51,
    60–61, 72, 79–80, 89, 92–93,
    104, 114, 116–117, 127–129,
    134, 138–140, 144
Socialist Party, vii, 8, 14, 19,
    27–28, 134, 139–140
Solidarity, 7, 12, 21, 55, 57, 61,
    64, 72, 81, 101, 113, 119, 127
Soviet Union, 22, 24, 28, 31, 50,
    52, 63, 80, 116, 140
Stalin, Joseph, 60
State, 3, 9, 16, 18–19, 25–26,
    29–31, 39–40, 43, 52, 54,

58–60, 62, 64, 66–73, 75, 78, 85–87, 92, 96, 100–101, 103, 113, 117–118, 122, 125, 129, 132–133, 137, 143–144
Sweden, 114, 116

Terra, Gabriel, 8–9, 15, 18–19, 21, 138
The Economist, 103
Topolansky, Lucía, 3–6, 87, 108–109, 134, 136, 138, 142, 144–145
Tupamaro, 3, 6, 36, 44–48, 50–51, 99, 118, 127

UNASUR, 67, 83, 139

United Nations, vi, 3, 118, 121, 123
University, vi, 3, 13–17, 30, 34, 97, 101–102, 107, 110, 112, 123, 130, 140
Uruguayan national anthem, 30

Vázquez, Tabaré, 3–5, 57–58, 81–82, 84, 90, 93, 97–98, 108, 125, 132, 134, 139, 143–144
Venezuela, 34, 50, 104, 135
Vertical, 35, 69
Vidart, Daniel, 1, 44
Vierci, Pablo, 4

Walsh, Rodolfo, 24, 139

www.ingramcontent.com/pod-product-compliance
Lightning Source LLC
Chambersburg PA
CBHW050610280326
41932CB00016B/2989